Andy Lakey's Psychomanteum
Spiritual Journeys Guided by Art, Angels and Miracles

Front cover art: *Reunions* by Andy Lakey 1997
In collection of Keith and Francesca Richardson

Back cover art: *The Cosmos* by Andy Lakey 1997
In collection of the artist

Printed in the United States of America

ISBN 0-9661555-0-5

Published by Ventura Press, P.O. Box 662, Ventura, CA 93002-662

Dedication

In loving memory of my mother, Marguerite, whose love for Andy Lakey's art and angels inspired me to write this book.

Acknowledgments

This book is the product of God, His angels and the many important people in my life. I could never have written this book without having an angel store. I thank my parents Kenneth and Marguerite Richardson for having the confidence to financially support our efforts to establish our unique theme store, even when they thought we were crazy and could not possibly succeed.

I wish to give a world of love and thanks to my wife Francesca for keeping the faith and for believing in God and His angels even when I had lost my faith. It was Francesca's spirituality and vision that made everything magical happen in our store and that continues to bring love and happiness into my life.

I am grateful to my sons Keith William and Kevin who have sacrificed their social lives and even some career opportunities to keep our store going. Their lives were touched by angels in the process. Their affiliation with our store has brought them renewed spirituality and confirmed their belief in God and His angels.

To Andy Lakey I give my heartfelt thanks and warmest regards. Andy is more than a business associate, he's a true friend. Andy's art, angels and miracles have taught me a great deal about the value of spirituality. Andy has truly been touched by angels. And his works have opened my eyes and allowed me to find the true meaning of God and His angels.

Finally, I wish to thank my editor, Mary Embree. Mary's enthusiasm and belief in my angel stories gave me further incentive to complete this book. Her fine editing and writing suggestions have made this book a truly wonderful, well-written work of art.

Contents

Foreword

In July of 1995, my administrative assistant gave me a cryptic note from Keith Richardson, a person I had never heard of. Keith owned an obscure Angel store in Ventura, California, a city I had never visited. He told my assistant he wanted to sell my art. I get hundreds of requests like this each year and usually turn them down.

As I already had over a hundred galleries selling my art throughout the world, I had no intention of opening a new art gallery. This was more work than my small staff and I could handle. For some reason, however, I felt guided by God. Something made me think that this message from Keith was important. Some divine force was urging me to call him back. I had received messages like this before and knew I had to follow God's directions.

At first I was not very positive about selling my art to him but I called him anyway. I had heard of his store, but hadn't seen it. I wasn't very impressed with what I had heard about it.

Keith told me of his family's strange encounter with The Virgin of Guadalupe (the patron saint of Mexico) and that he felt God's angels had guided him and his family to open their angel store.

Keith seemed very sincere and his story was quite compelling. I felt drawn to Keith's and his family's mission and decided to give them the opportunity to prove their sincerity by making their store one of my art galleries.

I didn't know it at the time, but my chance encounter with Keith was to change my life, my art, and the lives of thousands of people forever.

Within days of getting three small paintings in his store, Keith and his wife Francesca began noticing and documenting strange occurrences related to my art. I had been told of such events in the past, but never had they happened with such regularity, nor were they documented so thoroughly.

I am neither a psychic nor a prophet and I don't claim to know what the messages emanating from my art mean. I am just as surprised as anyone else when I get the reports of the angel paintings' messages. My personal belief is that I came back from a near death experience in 1986 with the ability to channel God's love through my art.

These messages often come to me like a laser beam as I paint them on my canvases. The messages people receive from my art are very consistent. They always bring love, hope and understanding to those whose lives they touch.

My angel paintings seem to increase the viewers' spirituality and guide them toward their higher purpose. In his book, *Andy Lakey's Psychomanteum,* Keith Richardson describes how my art, angels and miracles have changed his life and the lives of many others.

~ Andy Lakey

Preface

Our Psychomanteum

In the autumn of 1995, we built an art gallery in what used to be the storage room for our little store, *Things from Heaven,* on Main Street in Ventura, California.

There we hung pictures of angels painted by Andy Lakey. Right after customers started visiting the gallery and passing their hands across the paintings, strange things began happening. They told us that they felt a warmth and tingling in their hands and then a sense of peace and comfort would come over them. Some even began to get messages from the other side.

At first we dismissed these reported events as hallucinations, symptoms of extreme grief or even mental illness. But after seeing it happen again and again with people of all ages, races, religions and cultural backgrounds, we became convinced that something quite real and otherworldly was taking place.

One of our customers lent me a copy of *Reunions,* a book by Raymond A. Moody, M.D. In his book, Dr. Moody, who is best known for his work in bringing scientific validation to near death experiences, tells of his quest to study and build grief centers he calls *Psychomanteums.* He writes that Psychomanteums were established in ancient Greece as a divination tool. They were also credited with helping people deal with grief caused by the loss of loved ones. The Greek Psychomanteums consisted of clear pools of water that the griever could stare into and receive messages from the other side.

Dr. Moody has constructed his Psychomanteums using dimly lighted rooms with a mirror as a focal point. As many as 80% of the people entering these chambers experience reunions with loved ones that help them with grief-related issues.

~ ~ ~

Many of our customers have experienced inspiration, comfort and enlightenment through visiting our gallery. Others seem to have come to terms with their grief and found a way to begin their lives anew after losing a loved one.

We did not intend to establish a grief center. Indeed we had never before heard of such a thing. But we feel that we have been directed by angels to establish a Psychomanteum in our store.

This book is about our spiritual path and the power of angels. It's about our own unique Psychomanteum and the wonderful experiences and inspiring stories of those who have visited it.

Chapter One

Our Story

Being a logical thinker, I never intended to write a book like this. I was always taught to put my faith in the physical world and to believe there was a scientific explanation for everything. To my mind, people who promoted God, angels or religion were just confused or caught up in some kind of wishful thinking.

My university degrees were in anthropology and psychology. Armed with this practical education, I did anthropological field research in Nicaragua, Central America in 1976-77. My topic was the psychological relationship between religion and culture. I spent most of my time studying Virgin Mary cults and was amazed by how people could be taken in by such shallow religious practices.

In 1976, I published an article about ritual and culture in the scholarly journal *California Folklore.* Prior to this I had given presentations before the American Anthropology Association and the California Anthropology Association. For the next eighteen years, I used my logic and scientific knowledge to do market research, fundraising, and public relations for hospital systems. I earned certificates from the University of Southern California and San Jose State University in these fields.

My task was to upgrade the images of client organizations, and I managed to raise millions of dollars for new programs and construction of medical centers. Although the outcomes of some of my fundraising campaigns were nothing short of miraculous, I felt I deserved all the credit for success. I would have thought it was absurd to credit God or His angels. Nothing in all my research, studies or career prepared me for what has happened in my life in recent years.

My first wake-up call came in 1986 at the shrine of the Virgin of Guadalupe in Mexico City. A miracle happened that changed my spiritual life and led me to the path I walk today.

My second wake-up call came in 1995. This one led to my opening an angel store in Ventura, California. It also led me to meet the artist Andy Lakey and to experience the magic, mystery and spirituality of his art. My experiences with Lakey and his art have been so consistent and have occurred with such regularity that I felt compelled to write about them in this book.

Andy Lakey's Psychomanteum describes my family's spiritual journey and the way that Andy Lakey's art, angels and miracles touched our lives. I pray that reading this book will strengthen your spirituality and give you new hope and understanding of the power of God and His angels.

Our Spiritual Background

My parents did not go to church and I grew up without religious training. Although I attended Baptist Sunday school as a child and belonged to a Methodist youth group as a teenager, I never attended church regularly and was never baptized.

My wife Francesca, on the other hand, had a strong religious background. She grew up in a small town in Nicaragua, where she went to a Roman Catholic girls school and attended church regularly. Francesca's parents reinforced her beliefs, and were part of their community's Roman Catholic faithful. She grew up firmly believing in God, angels and miracles.

As a young woman, Francesca excelled so much in her spiritual faith that she was chosen by church officials to enter a convent for training as a nun. But because she was their oldest daughter, Francesca's parents did not allow her to pursue religious training. They wanted her to marry and have children.

In 1972, they sent her to the United States to further her education and to get her away from a boyfriend of whom they disapproved. It was here that we met. She was staying with her brother, Rennie Quesada, who was a friend of mine. At first our relationship consisted only of smiles and glances because we didn't know each other's language. By 1974, Francesca's English and my Spanish had improved enough that things started to change.

Francesca and I started dating and by 1975 decided to get married. To meet her religious needs and to please her family, Francesca wanted to be married in the Roman Catholic faith. But we found that wasn't possible because I was divorced. I'd had a brief, unhappy marriage some years before just after I had gotten out of the Navy.

To the Roman Catholic Church, this was an unforgivable mistake. We met with four different priests in various churches, all of whom told us the same thing. Francesca should find another man to marry. I was unworthy of the church's marital blessing and they considered our relationship to be sinful.

We were eventually married by a Methodist minister in his church. Francesca was so hurt by the cold, uncaring attitude of the Roman Catholic priests that she gave up her religious faith altogether. For the next eleven years we lived with no God, no angels and no religion in our home.

Our Message from The Virgin of Guadalupe

In 1986, we went to Mexico City on vacation and a series of miraculous events occurred. Before we left, a friend of mine asked if I could light a candle for her sick mother at the shrine of Virgin of Guadalupe and I agreed.

The Virgin of Guadalupe is the patron saint of Mexico. She is famous for performing thousands of curative miracles throughout the world. The 460-year-old shroud that hangs in her shrine is a miracle itself. In 1531, Juan Diego, an Aztec Indian who had converted to Christianity, climbed a hill near Mexico City. There he saw a vision of the Virgin Mary who told Juan to bring a message to the Bishop of Mexico City. The message was to build a church at the top of the hill.

Faithfully, Juan walked the three miles to the cathedral and asked the guards at the gate if he could have a hearing. After waiting all day Juan was finally greeted by a very skeptical bishop.

"I can't go building churches everywhere the Indians tell me to," the bishop said. "You'll need to bring me proof if you expect me to believe you actually spoke with the Virgin Mary."

Several days later, Juan returned to the hilltop where he had seen the vision. Again he saw the Virgin Mary. He told her the bishop required more proof. It was December 12, and she gave him a bundle of roses, which do not bloom at that time of year in Mexico City. Juan put the roses in his *tilma* (cloak) and returned to the cathedral.

When he met with the bishop, Juan opened his *tilma*. The cleric was impressed by the roses, but even more so by what he saw on Juan's *tilma.* Embossed therein was a beautiful portrait of the Virgin Mary. As there was no known technology to produce such a work of art at that time, it was immediately declared a miracle.

In the late 19th Century, Roman Catholic Church leaders tired to debunk some of the fake miracles to which church members had clung. The Virgin of Guadalupe was on their list. Juan's *tilma* was subjected to a rigorous scientific study.

When it was magnified, scientists found to their shock that inside the pupils of the Virgin Mary's eyes was a reflection of the Indian Juan Diego. They concluded this was truly a miracle. The only way reflections like these could have occurred would be in a photograph, and photographs were not invented until 400 years after the *tilma's* appearance.

My family arrived at the shrine on a cool July afternoon. We bought a candle to light at the altar for my friend's mother. It occurred to me that my friend would appreciate photographs of our religious vigil. I took pictures of my sons buying the candle, putting the candle on the altar, and lighting it. As an afterthought, I photographed the *tilma*. I took two photos; one from the right side and one from the left.

When we returned home, I had my film developed. The day I picked up the prints, I discovered to my shock that from my roll of 36 pictures, I had only one photo that faced the wrong direction. It was one of the two photos of the *tilma*. We showed it to film experts, who were baffled. That only one photo from a full roll would turn out backwards was perplexing. And why would it be the *tilma* of The Virgin of Guadalupe? Furthermore, color film cannot be developed when negatives are reversed. Several religious authorities with whom we discussed this could not explain it either.

"This is your miracle," they told us. "You'll have to find out for yourselves what it means."

For Francesca, who was raised in a culture accustomed to miracles, it made sense. I, however, had been raised with a logical, no-nonsense approach to the world, and it all seemed a little crazy to me.

Our Lessons in Kansas

Within months of our Mexico trip, I was recruited by a national executive search firm to take a job as director of fundraising and marketing. This job was with a national Episcopal mental health organization based in Salina, Kansas. The position had been held by an Episcopal priest for the previous forty years, and I was concerned about the religious nature of the job. Although I turned it down three times, in the end I was offered everything I asked for and felt obligated to accept.

~ ~ ~

Once I took the job, power, abundance and prestige seemed to come to us. We sold our small townhouse in San Jose, California and bought a beautiful four-acre country estate in Kansas. Francesca and I joined the Episcopal Church. Our children and I were baptized and Francesca was received. I was elected a member of the Vestry at the Episcopal Cathedral. Francesca was elected president of the Episcopal Church Women.

We felt this was our calling and that this was what the

miracle of the Virgin Mary photos was about. We were wrong. It was only a lesson. After less than two years in this ideal position, things began to go wrong. The priest who had recruited and hired me was fired and a new priest was hired to oversee the organization. The new priest was one of the least spiritual people I had ever met. He demonstrated how one can find a great deal of religion and have no spirituality at all.

Although he pretended to be a most kind and religious person, I found him to be very deceitful and manipulative. His management style consisted of threats, humiliation and lies.

Even though my work had helped triple the organization's funds raised and doubled full-fee admissions, the new priest believed that my position should be filled by an Episcopal priest. He made my life miserable for the next two years. And when I did not quit, he fired me.

How We Found Grace

I launched a nationwide job search, sent out hundreds of resumes and interviewed for dozens of jobs, but I couldn't find work, and we returned to California. My parents suggested we move near them, so we settled in the coastal city of Oxnard, about an hour north of Los Angeles.

I was eventually offered what seemed the opportunity of a lifetime. A Los Angeles man with powerful political ties in Mexico offered me a full partnership in an international trade organization. I took the position and arranged hundreds of trade agreements between U.S. and international markets. In the end however, I was cheated and slandered by my partner. I lost everything—my career, my good name and my financial stability.

My family was in dire straits. We were on the verge of becoming homeless and our credit was destroyed. I applied for public assistance and we received welfare and food stamps. We rented out two rooms in our own rented property so we could afford to live there. I continued to look for employment, but found none.

Seeing the gravity of our situation, my father tried to help. Two of his friends sat on the board of a local charity, and they needed someone to establish a thrift shop for their organization.

My father told them I had over twenty years experience with nonprofit organizations and had established several thrift shops. They requested a proposal and I produced one. Although they said the project was in committee and they would get back to me when a decision was made, they never did.

With my father's backing of a $5,000 loan, I began to look for a place in the community to establish my thrift shop. My research pointed to Main Street in downtown Ventura, near our home in Oxnard, as the best place.

That's where Francesca and I began looking for a vacant storefront in summer 1994. Nothing was available even after several months, and we became more and more discouraged. It looked as though there was no hope for us.

Francesca's Message from Heaven

Francesca began having strange, recurring dreams where she would find herself walking outside and looking skyward. Then the clouds would open to reveal hundreds of beautiful angels. She would look at them and smile, and the angels would smile back at her, but no one spoke.

These dreams continued until January 1995, when she began to see something different. Alejandro Figueroa, a childhood friend from Nicaragua who had died the previous year, came to Francesca with a beautiful gold-bound book.

"What are you doing here, Alejandro?" Francesca asked, surprised. "You're supposed to be dead."

"I know I'm dead, but I've been sent to bring you this book."

"What kind of book is this?" she asked.

"Read the book with me and find out."

Alejandro opened the golden book. It was full of information about angels. Francesca read the following passages:

"Angels are beings of light."

"Angels are messengers of God."

"Angels bring God's love to the world."

She read the entire book in her dream. At about five a.m. she woke me to tell me about it. She went on and on until I finally told her to go back to sleep. I was sure the stress of our financial condition was getting to her and she was starting to imagine things.

Later at breakfast with our two sons, Keith and Kevin, Francesca enthusiastically related her dream.

Kevin, our youngest, who was thirteen at the time, shook his head and said, "No, Mom. I don't think so, Mom!"

"What is this, Kevin?" Francesca became defensive. "First your father doesn't want to hear about my dream. Now you don't want to hear about it."

"It isn't that I don't want to hear about it," Kevin said. "It's that you can't do what you said you did. You can't read in a dream."

Kevin continued. "One side of your brain reads and the other side dreams. You can't do both at the same time. Either you didn't read the book or it wasn't a dream."

Francesca and I stared at each other. We knew Kevin was right but we could not explain what had happened.

"I know I read the book," Francesca said. "I remember what I read."

With that, she again began quoting the things she had read.

"'Angels are messengers of God. They're beings of light. They bring God's love to the world.' I really know what I read!"

Later that day we again walked down Main Street searching for a site for our proposed thrift store. To our surprise, we found a storefront with a "for lease" sign in the window. The landlord's office was around the corner, so we went there and spoke to his representative. He was anxious to have someone lease the property.

The storefront was in the worst part of downtown Ventura. There was an abandoned liquor store and a 24-hour porno store on one side, and a struggling antique shop operated by a part-time merchant on the other. Upstairs was a transient hotel. The awning hung in shreds. Street people who were living in the recessed entrance to the small shop were begging us for money.

The inside was worse. The building had most recently been used as a drug rehabilitation recreation center. Rotting couches lined both sides of the wall for about 50 feet. The carpet was hidden under a two-inch layer of cigarette butts. The place had recently been fumigated, and dead rats and cockroaches were spread among the cigarettes. As we walked further into the building, things got even worse.

The back room was filled, floor to ceiling, with broken furniture, rotting carpets and old mattresses. At the very back were washing machines, dryers and piles of dirty clothes. The restroom walls were slathered with black moss. The restroom light fixture was full of water from ceiling leaks.

Francesca looked at this hopeless mess, this renovation disaster, and announced, "This is perfect. This is where we're supposed to be. We're not supposed to have a thrift shop. We're supposed to have an angel store here. That's what my dream was all about."

I disagreed.

"We don't know anything about running a retail gift store," I pointed out. "We don't know where to purchase angel gifts. We don't know how to display angel gifts.

And we don't know how much to sell angel gifts for."

"We can learn," Francesca replied. "I got a message from God to open this store. We need to do what God wants us to do."

There was no arguing with her. When Francesca makes up her mind about something, there's nothing any-one can do to change it.

To help me complete the lease negotiations, I called my father. We negotiated a very fair agreement with the building owner. He gave us two months free rent so we could refurbish the building.

After the lease had been settled, my father asked me about our thrift shop and how we were going to bring in a local charity to be our sponsor.

"We've changed our minds," I explained. "Instead of a thrift shop, we're going to open an angel store."

"A what?" my father replied.

"An angel store," I answered.

"What in the hell is an angel store?" he asked.

"It's a store where we will sell all kinds of angel gifts," I explained timidly.

"Like knickknacks?" he asked.

"Yes, like knickknacks."

"Well, let me get this straight," he continued. "You

want to have a knickknack store that sells only one type of knickknack."

"Yes, that's correct," I responded.

"Well, that's about the dumbest idea I ever heard of in my entire life," he answered. "You guys are going to go bankrupt and be living on the street in just a few months. And I'm going to get stuck with all the lease payments. I'm not going to lend you any money if you don't give up the stupid idea of having an angel store."

I explained that Francesca had made her mind up and wanted an angel store or nothing. After further discussion, we finally compromised. My father would lend us $5,000 to get the store started, if we changed the store's focus from selling angels to selling food.

"Sell a few angel gifts if that appeases Francesca," he said. "But don't make angels your store's major product or I'm sure you'll fail."

Things from Heaven - An Angel Store

We opened our store April 1, 1995 with little fanfare. The original name of our business was *Things from Heaven - Food and Gifts*. We had no sign, no telephone and we did no advertising. Those were luxuries requiring money we did not have.

We found right away that our customers were not interested in food. It just gathered dust on the shelves. They were only interested in our angels. Within several months, we closed out all the food and sold only angel gifts. We also changed our store's name to *Things from Heaven - An Angel Store*.

Two months later, in June 1995, Monsignor O'Brien from the nearby San Buenaventura Mission came to bless our store. He told us that the land our building occupied had once been the mission gardens.

Once the store was blessed, magical things began to occur. When we placed our two photos of the Virgin of Guadalupe on the shelf of an ugly old cabinet, it bloomed into a spontaneous downtown shrine. Visitors to the store began to write messages on little pieces of paper and put them on the cabinet around the pictures. Today people come from miles away to pray and write notes to God and place them on that shrine.

~ ~ ~

The most important thing to happen however, was the arrival of Andy Lakey's art in our store. I myself stood in the way of this event three times, but I could not stop it. When something is God's will, nothing can prevent it.

Andy Lakey's art, angels and miracles have greatly influenced our store's success and changed my family's life forever.

Chapter Two

Messages from Heaven

Andy Lakey was not trained to be an artist, nor did he want to be one. He sold cars and used his money to buy drugs. He prided himself on the quality of his cocaine. He didn't care about anyone or anything.

On December 31, 1986, Lakey went to a New Year's Eve party. There he 'free-based' cocaine. As the evening went on, he began to feel worse and worse. He felt as if his head was going to explode and his whole body was shutting down.

He didn't tell his friends how bad he felt. He thought he was too 'cool' to overdose. Quietly leaving the party, he headed for his apartment downstairs. By the time he got there, he was crawling on his hands and knees. He crawled into the shower, turned the cold water on himself, and prayed for the first time since he was eight years old.

"God if you spare my life," he said, "I'll never take drugs again and I'll do something to help humankind."

Feeling something swirling around his feet like a tornado, he looked down, and to his amazement saw seven glowing beings of light circling his body. The beings shone like the sun and looked like they were made of crystal. They came up to his chest and put their arms around him. Suddenly, Lakey felt at peace. He knew he had been saved by angels.

In this near-death experience, Lakey was surrounded by seven angels, saw the light of God, and glimpsed the 'other side.' After he recovered, he stopped taking drugs cold turkey, began helping other people, and became obsessed with drawing what he had seen that night in his shower.

Lakey quit his job, moved out of his apartment and left all his friends. He found a new job and a new place to live. Instead of taking drugs each night when he came home, he drew pictures of his near-death experience. This continued for three years, by which time Lakey had boxes full of sketches.

In October 1989, Lakey, obsessed by a feeling that he wasn't doing what he was supposed to do, quit his $85,000-a-year sales job, took all his savings out of the bank and bought $6,000 worth of art supplies. He felt compelled to paint the images he had seen in the shower.

He built an art studio, but when he sat down to paint he discovered something terribly wrong. He had no art training and didn't have the slightest idea how to make paint stick to the canvas. He would start at the top and the paint would drip down to the bottom. No matter how he tried, everything he created looked like mud.

Several discouraging months passed, and then one morning in early 1990, as he entered his studio, a beam of light shone through the wall and touched him on the forehead. He felt a tingling sensation run through his entire body. Lakey felt transported to another dimension—a dimension where time stood still.

Three angels appeared and said, "The reason you were spared is that you have a mission to fulfill."

He asked them what his mission was and they responded, "Your mission is to paint 2,000 individual angel paintings by the year 2000. These paintings will represent each year that has passed since the birth of Christ."

"But I can't do that," Lakey interrupted. "You know I can't paint."

"Don't worry about a thing," they reassured him. "Put it in our hands and we'll take care of everything for you."

Within 24 hours, Lakey experienced a series of coincidences that would forever change his life. First, he accidentally spilled two acrylic paints that, when mixed, dried to a hard puffed surface. This novel mix of materials led Lakey to an art style known as 'sensualism.' As the paintings he created had a textured surface, even blind people could "see" them with their fingers. This new style caused ripples in the art world and brought a new level of spirituality to many who came in contact with it.

In just a few months, Lakey had a full gallery opening. Six hundred people attended and his exhibit sold out. One buyer was a vacationing Italian Monsignor. Upon his return home, he spread the word about Lakey's angel paintings and within weeks Lakey got a call from the Vatican. Pope John Paul II wanted a painting. Lakey sent the Pope painting number one in his 2000 series.

Today, Andy Lakey is the world's most famous living angel artist. His works hang in museums and art galleries around the world. Noted collectors include Princess Margaret of Great Britain, Prince Albert of Monaco, King Hussein of Jordan, Presidents Ford and Carter, Ray Charles, Stevie Wonder, Quincy Jones, Shari Belafonte, James Redfield, Betty Eadie, Ed Asner, Patty Duke, Kelsey Grammar, Naomi Judd, General Chuck Yeager,

Mickey Mantel, Arnold Palmer and Dudley Moore.

Despite his fame, Lakey has remained true to his mission. He donates at least 30% of the money from everything he paints to help others. He supports The Blind Children's Center in Los Angeles and other children's charities throughout the world. Lakey is also a supporter of charities for abused women, AIDS research and animal welfare.

Andy Lakey's art has touched millions of lives. It continues to help people find faith, hope and spirituality, and to face life's tragedies. His art has been a major factor in my family's spiritual journey. The magic and mystery of Lakey's art has changed our lives and those of many others who have visited our angel store, *Things from Heaven*.

Chapter Three

How Angels Brought Us Lakey's Art

It was May 1995, and we had been open only 30 days when a very striking woman named Pam came in. She was in her early forties and had jet black hair and piercing gray-blue eyes. From the beginning, Pam was impressed with our endeavor.

"I love your store," she said. "I love everything here. I love the energy of this store. I love you guys. You should sell international art in this store."

I try to look at things from a realistic point of view. I knew we had started our store with an investment of only $5,000, and the place was a disaster. Our shelves were bare. A curtain hung across the center. We didn't have anything for sale that cost more than $30.

Furthermore, downtown Ventura was a disaster. During the first 30 days we were open the city initiated a downtown revitalization effort. They cut down all the trees, tore out the sidewalks and closed the streets. With the exception of the homeless people who lived in the park across the street, few customers came in. I told Pam we were not quite ready for international art yet.

"You should be selling artist Andy Lakey's paintings in your store," she continued, undaunted.

"Who's Andy Lakey?" I asked.

"He's the most famous living angel artist. His art hangs in the Vatican. He's been on many television programs including *Sightings* and *Angels: The Mysterious Messengers.*"

I told Pam I had seen Lakey on *Sightings* but I didn't think our store was ready for his art yet.

"I disagree with you," she persisted. "I know you're wrong. Your store is ready for Andy's art and you have to call him and get his art in your store right now."

Pam made me promise that I would call. I did not take her seriously. The whole thing was unrealistic, and I never bothered to make the call.

Two months later Pam returned. She marched right up to me and asked, "Have you called Andy yet?"

"Andy who?" I said.

"Andy Lakey, the artist I told you about the last time I

was here," she replied. "You've got to call him right now!"

"I appreciate your interest," I responded. "But let's be realistic. There are hundreds of beautiful gift shops in California where an artist like Andy Lakey could sell his art. There are hundreds of beautiful galleries in California. Why would an internationally known artist of his stature want to put his art in our store?"

"Look, I love everything about your store," Pam continued as though she hadn't heard me. "And Andy Lakey's a friend of mine. I worked with him ten years ago. When I saw Andy last week, I told him about you and he said he might be interested in having his art in your store. You've got to call him. You've got to call him right now!"

"Do you have his phone number?" I asked.

"No," she demurred.

"Do you know where his studio is?"

"No."

"I'll contact Lakey when I get time," I said.

Pam looked sad and confused.

She said, "I'm not leaving this store until you call Andy Lakey!"

Now I was concerned that I truly was in the presence

of some kind of mental case. I considered calling 911 to get the police to take her away. At that very moment, I noticed my copy of *Angel Times Magazine* on the counter. The cover advertised an article about Andy Lakey.

Grabbing it, I opened it up, and there on the inside cover was a toll free phone number—1(800) LAKEY ART. I had nothing to lose. I called and got an art gallery in New York State and asked to speak to Andy Lakey.

"Andy Lakey isn't here," I was told. "Andy doesn't live in New York. He lives in California."

The voice on the other end of the line gave me Lakey's California office number. I called and spoke to his assistant.

"I can't be very encouraging about allowing you to sell Andy's art in your store," she said.

I told her about Pam, that she used to work with Andy and she suggested I call.

Andy's assistant said, "I'm sure Andy will appreciate your interest, but we have over 100 galleries around the world and I know he has no intention of opening any new ones in the near future."

I thanked her and began to lower the phone to hang up when she said, "Wait! If you'd like, I'll take your name and number and someday, if we ever decide to open another gallery, we'll call you."

This is really a waste of my time, I thought to myself. I was about to tell her to forget it when I looked up at Pam. She was looking right through me with her cold gray-blue eyes. If I don't leave my name and number, I thought to myself, Pam will be in here every week driving me crazy.

I left the information, and two days later Lakey called.

"I've heard of your store and I might have some interest in having my art there," he said. "But I have some major concerns."

I thought to myself, my God, if he's really heard of my store, he knows what bad shape we're in.

"What are your concerns, Andy?"

"My major concern is I don't know where Ventura is. Where is your store in relation to San Mateo and San Juan Capistrano?" (Those were two other California cities where there were galleries carrying his paintings.)

I assured him we were very far from both places. We talked for about an hour and when we were done we had a deal. I had to purchase three paintings right away. I did not actually have the money, so I used the rent. We put the three paintings at the back of the store and began to take orders.

Lakey and I didn't meet until March 1996, almost a year later. My wife and I went to his studio in Murrieta, California. While we were there, we talked about a number of things.

Finally he asked, "Could you refresh my memory and tell me how I came to sell art in your store?"

I reminded him about his friend Pam, and how it was due to her persistence we had been led to do business together. He shook his head and said, "No! That's not what really happened. That's not how I remember it at all."

"What do you think happened?" I asked.

"The way I remember it," Lakey responded, "the angels brought you to me. The angels bring everything to me."

I smiled. "Maybe you can say something like that on television or to the tabloid newspapers, but not to me. I know what really happened."

"What do you think really happened, Keith?" Andy said, smiling.

"What really happened is your good friend Pam, whose opinion you apparently respect, told you about our store and you decided to give us a try on her recommendation."

"There's something you should know about Pam,"

Lakey told me. "She's not a good friend of mine. In fact, I hadn't seen her in ten years when we met several months ago and she told me about your store. Hundreds of people tell me about places I should display my art every day, and I don't act on it. But when I learned about your store, I felt I had been given a message from God. And these messages are never wrong. I have to do what God tells me."

"What do you mean by that?" I asked.

Andy continued, "I know it was divine intervention because when I acted on the message, you began selling more of my art than any other store in the entire world."

To this day, *Things from Heaven*, in its unlikely location in downtown Ventura, is Andy Lakey's number one gallery for volume and total dollar sales. More people own Andy Lakey's art in Ventura County than in any other county.

Things from Heaven has recently been selected by Lakey as one of his three major studios in the world. Here he plans to paint as many as twenty paintings each month.

Wow, There's an Energy!

We had been selling Lakey's paintings for just over a week when a very conservative looking woman in her early seventies with blue-gray hair came in. She was dressed in a navy blue pinstriped pantsuit and carried herself with an air of dignity. She appeared to have the financial means to make a major purchase, so I showed her the three small Lakey paintings we owned. As I did, I ran my hand about an inch above a painting to describe its unique style and details.

At that moment, I experienced something beyond logic or reason. I felt heat, and a tingling sensation similar to having pins vibrating all over the palm of my hand.

Wow, I thought to myself, I really felt that. I can't believe this is happening to me. I knew if I said anything the conservative customer would leave the store in a hurry. So I played it cool. I slowly lowered my hand, put it behind my back and stepped away from the painting.

The woman reached up and put her hand near the same spot. She flicked her hand away as if from a hot stove.

"Did you feel that?" she asked me.

"Feel what?" I responded cautiously.

"The heat and the tingling coming off this painting," she replied.

"Yes, I did," I replied timidly.

"What is it?!" she asked.

"I don't know," I answered. "They didn't tell me these paintings did that."

For the next two days, I had everyone who came in the store run their hands over the paintings. Eight of ten people felt the heat and tingling. I called Lakey's office to find out what was happening. His assistant knew nothing about the phenomenon, but she suggested I call the writer Paul Robert Walker who was in the process of completing Lakey's first book, *Andy Lakey: Art, Angels and Miracles.* She said Paul had done a great deal of research about Andy's art and knew everything about phenomena occurring around it.

I called Paul, introduced myself to him and told him what had been happening.

"Is this a local phenomenon caused by power lines under my store?" I asked, and then added jokingly, "Is this phenomenon caused by the spiritual grid that runs from Ojai to the Channel Islands?" (Local folklore holds that a strange energy field exists between Ojai, a nearby town, and some islands off the coast.)

"This isn't an isolated incident," Paul said. "Nor a local phenomenon. I'm getting reports about this same thing from all over the United States and around the world. In fact, when Shari Belafonte hosted a segment of *Lifestyles of the Rich and Famous* in 1994, she was so amazed by her experience with some of the Lakey paintings' energy that she wrote a chapter in my new book about it."

"I remember feeling this sensation up my arm, whoo-oo-oo, like a burst of energy," Belafonte had written. "And I remember thinking that's the difference ... that's what's really special about this artist."

Since this initial experience, Francesca and I have invited thousands of people from around the world to experience the energy of the paintings. They include Roman Catholic priests and nuns, Pentecostal church groups, Russian diplomats, international tourists and even a Tibetan Sherpa.

The Paintings Know Where They Belong

As soon as we received our first three paintings, strange things began to happen. Within minutes of hanging them, a customer named Aquariana entered. She was thin with terminal cancer, her skin was pale and pasty and she walked with a limp. She claimed to have psychic abilities and did palm readings at a local coffee house, priding herself on using a Bible to find answers to people's problems. Closing her eyes, she ran her hand about an inch above one of the paintings.

"These paintings are very spiritual and each has its own special purpose," she said.

The first painting she moved her hand over was a 6-by-8-inch picture of a pink angel and four rays of light.

"This painting has a child's energy," she said. "It should be in a child's room. It would help a child find spirituality."

The next was a blue 8-by-10-inch painting with three angels and five rays of light.

"This painting is for group healing," Aquariana said. "It would help members of a youth group find peace and understanding in their lives."

She then ran her hand over the third painting, which was 6 by 8 inches and depicted two angels and four rays of light.

"This is the most spiritual painting of all," she said. "This painting will help people go to the other side in peace. It should go to a hospice."

Her analyses were interesting, although obviously not believable.

~~~

The next day a well-known psychic from Santa Barbara came to our store. He had heard we were selling Lakey's paintings and wanted to see them firsthand. I
~~~

couldn't resist questioning him about the meaning of each.

He closed his eyes and ran his hand over them.

He repeated almost word for word what Aquariana had said the day before.

One painting had a child's energy and was for a child's room. One had group energy and was for a youth group, and one would offer powerful help to the dying, so it should be hung in a hospice. The odds against these two separate predictions being exactly the same are small indeed. What was to happen later, however, was even more amazing.

We did not tell anyone about these predictions. In fact, these paintings were originally intended for display only. We took orders for commissioned and spiritual energy paintings, and after we began to see a little profit come in from orders, we ordered more. Only at that point did we begin selling art from the store's walls.

The first painting of the three to sell was the one purported to have a 'child's energy.' A young man whose wife was pregnant with their first child said he felt there was something about it that would help his baby find spirituality. He purchased the painting for his child's room.

The next to go was the one we had been told would help people face their deaths in a hospice. It was purchased by members of a local senior citizens group. The group meets weekly to discuss spiritual issues. The group leader—to whom we had divulged nothing about the psychics' predictions—said he felt the painting might help group members' face their deaths with more peace and understanding.

The sale of the third painting, predicted to hold group energy, made me question the validity of psychic predictions. A woman suffering from cancer purchased it, saying that it helped her more than all her cancer medications combined. She ran her hand over it and reported feeling peace and comfort, as well as a powerful sort of energy. For me, her purchase proved that the other two sales were just a coincidence.

About a month later, she returned to our store. Lakey had just sent us a new and striking spiritual energy painting depicting "The Virgin of Guadalupe." The woman seemed obsessed with the new painting. It really called to her and made her feel even better than the other one. We agreed to trade the painting she had previously purchased for the new one.

We hung the "group energy" painting back up on the wall. Within two weeks, a representative of a local youth group purchased it. All three paintings had indeed been sold as the two psychics foretold. I started to see that Lakey's art is not purchased at random. It goes to those who need it most.

Chapter Four

The Amazing Spiritual Energy Paintings

When I bought our first three Lakey paintings, I faced a major retail challenge. I wanted to sell them but I also needed to keep some on display in order to sell more. Lakey suggested I do what many of his other galleries were doing: commission "spiritual energy" paintings.

"What is a spiritual energy painting?" I naturally asked.

"I have the gift of feeling the energy from spiritual items," he explained. "Whenever I put a meaningful item behind one of my canvases, I pick up its energy and I paint what I receive.

"Spiritual energy is like a lake, I reach in and grab some of it and put it on the canvas. I never know what I am going to paint. Collectors are always amazed by the results."

"What kinds of items can we use?" I wondered.

"It can be almost anything," he said. "It can be a photograph, a letter, a fingerprint, an outline of someone's hand or any other thing that means something to your customer. There are only two limitations on spiritual energy materials people send me. First, I don't want any item that is larger than the canvas I'm going to paint. I'm afraid I might get paint on it. Second, I don't want anything that's irreplaceable, like expensive jewelry or family heirloom photographs. I'm afraid I might lose them."

We All Walk Different Paths

Our first request for a spiritual energy painting came from a Christian youth group leader named Arley. He and his group lived in a city about two hours away, and they had found our store while on a spiritual retreat in Ventura.

Arley commissioned an 8-by-10-inch painting. He gave me a photo of his entire group so Lakey could use its spiritual energy. Arley included a note requesting a painting that would enhance spirituality and healing within the group. I sent the photo and note to Lakey and about six weeks later I received Arley's painting.

It seemed so odd in style and format that I was concerned. It was unlike Lakey's other creations. Seven tiny golden angel figures each had a wavy line under them. They looked to me like small golden bugs surfing on seven wavy little surfboards. The more I studied it, the more concerned I became. I suspected Arley and his group would ask for their money back.

Arley and two assistants arrived on a Saturday morning. I showed them the painting making certain they saw their youth group photo taped behind it. Arley looked at it and then whispered something to one of the others. They passed it back and forth among the three of them. I became more and more concerned.

I asked myself why had I ever let Andy Lakey talk me into doing something as stupid as "spiritual energy" paintings.

My worst fears seemed confirmed. Arley and his assistants put their hands over their eyes and began to shake their heads back and forth.

"What did you tell Andy Lakey about our group?" Arley asked as he pointed at me.

Now I was on the defensive.

"All I told him was that you wanted a painting that would help with your group's spirituality and healing. If you're dissatisfied, I'll have Lakey paint you something else."

"But we love this painting!" Arley smiled. "We're totally amazed! We're blown away! How did Andy Lakey know our group's philosophy?" he asked. "Did you tell him?"

"I don't know anything about it. What is this philosophy anyway?" I asked.

"It's right here on our painting," Arley responded. "Don't you see it? We saw it right away"

"No," I said. "I don't see anything special at all."

"Every morning when we start our meeting, we tell our kids the same thing. 'We all walk different paths, but we're all are going to the same place, seven days a week.'"

Then I saw it clearly. There were seven little golden angels next to wavy lines, which represented the paths. They were all going to the same place. All the angels were headed toward the light of heaven.

Lakey had been right. His paintings did have special meaning. He really did paint with spiritual energy.

I have met with Arley several times since. He was so impressed that he commissioned spiritual energy paintings for his two sons and his daughter. He tells me the paintings continue to bring his children and his youth group renewed peace and increased spirituality.

Sky Diver Angel

In late 1995 a customer named Dorothy brought me one of the strangest photos I had ever seen—of someone free-falling from an airplane—and she commissioned a spiritual painting using it. She was secretive about the photo.

"This is something that has haunted me for a long time," Dorothy said. "I really can't tell you anything about it. I need to know 100 percent in my heart that Andy Lakey will paint with the spiritual energy of my photograph, and that you will not tell him anything."

I sent the photo out with Dorothy's order and about six weeks later the painting arrived. Nothing about it seemed unusual. It was 6 by 8 inches with one medium-sized angel flying upwards and six rays of light coming down. Wisps of white floated on a powder blue background. The number was 1,392 of Lakey's two thousand angel painting series. As I handed the painting to Dorothy, I questioned her again.

"You were very secretive about this photo. What is this of, anyway?"

"It's me. I'm a professional skydiver."

Dorothy is a tall, elegant woman and always stylishly dressed.

"You're a skydiver?" I said.

"I'm a professional photographer and I work with skydiving teams," she explained. "This photo was taken of me in 1992, when I was part of a six-member team."

She hesitated before continuing. "One day in 1992, my team was going to make a jump. I had a personal problem come up and had to take care of it. Someone else was hired to do the photography and jumped in my place. That day the plane crashed and everyone was killed. I'm the only survivor of our team."

"It's interesting that the painting has six rays of light, and there were six members in your team," I commented.

"Yes, there are six rays," Dorothy said. "But there are six rays of light on many of Lakey's paintings." She pointed to several examples on the gallery wall.

"Maybe you're right," I said.

I turned the painting over and looked at the number 1,392.

"Look at this," I said. "If you add up the numbers on the back—one, three, nine and two—they add up to fifteen. One and five make six again."

"I don't believe in numerology," Dorothy said and shook her head. "You can add numbers up all different ways and they really don't mean anything."

As I handed her the painting, she immediately placed her hand over it to feel the energy. Then she turned it over and looked at the numbers. She gasped and began to cry.

"Are you okay?" I asked.

"My God," she said. "The number of this painting is 13 - 92. Our plane crashed on the 13th, and the year of the accident was 1992."

Dorothy left and returned several months later with her husband.

"I want to thank you, and I want you to thank Andy Lakey for me," she said. "The painting you sold me has changed my life. Before I bought this painting, I had what is called 'survivor's syndrome.' I couldn't sleep at night, and I often found myself crying uncontrollably."

"Since I've had my Lakey painting, I've come to realize something. It was their time to go, and it wasn't my time to go."

"Whenever I'm feeling sad or lonely, or anytime something goes wrong in my life, I take my painting off my wall, run my hand over it and feel its energy. Then I know I'm here for a reason. I still have a mission to accomplish in my life."

~ ~ ~

Anasazi Angel

In early 1996, a customer named Janie brought me a photo that she wanted to be used for a spiritual energy painting. It was of a man dressed in a tuxedo with a Hawaiian Lei around his neck.

"This was taken at my wedding reception," Janie said. "I chose it because of the blue wispy cloud in the background. I recall no clouds like this on the day of the reception. I wondered how Andy Lakey would interpret it"

I assumed the man in the picture was Janie's husband, and sent if off to Lakey. About two months later Janie's painting was delivered. It was 8 by 10 inches with one angel flying up toward several light rays. The background was turquoise blue. At each corner was a spiral swirl and at the center of each side was a strange swiggle.

"Does this painting mean anything to you?" I asked Janie when she came in to pick it up.

"Nothing at all," she said.

"Isn't that your husband in the photo?"

"No," Janie replied, "That's a good friend of the family who attended our wedding. I wanted Lakey to do a spiritual energy painting because of the swirly blue cloud. I wondered if Lakey's painting could help me find the photo's meaning."

Janie left but called back several weeks later.

"I think I just figured out what my painting means," she said. "I was watching a special on PBS about the Anasazi Indians of the Southwestern United States and I realized the Anasazi spiritual symbols were the same as the symbols on my painting."

"What does this have to do with the photograph you gave me?"

"The man in the photo is an archeologist," Janie explained. "His main area of study is the Anasazi Indians. This man just planned a trip for my husband and me so we could see the best Anasazi sites during our vacation this summer."

When Janie and her husband returned from their vacation, she brought her painting back to the store along with a book on Anasazi symbolism that he had bought on the trip. She showed me the symbols in the book that almost exactly matched the symbols on her Lakey painting.

They were from an Anasazi calendar and included symbols for summer, spring, fall and winter. Janie was amazed by Lakey's portrayal of the calendar. She was also astonished that the painting was turquoise. Turquoise, she had discovered, was the major trade good of the Anasazi Indians.

Baseball Player Angel

In spring 1996, a tearful young woman named Cheryl brought a photo to us for a spiritual energy painting. It was on a baseball card and pictured her nephew Jason, a minor league player. Jason had died several months earlier in an automobile accident.

We sent Jason's card to Lakey and a couple of months later received back a beautiful blue and gold angel painting. Number 251 in Lakey's series, it featured eight rays of light and one angel going up.

As we looked at the painting we found everything added up to eight, including the rays of light and the painting number. We were especially surprised to see that the number on the baseball card was 26. Two and six also adds up to eight.

We also noticed that the colors on the baseball card were blue and gold, just like the painting. I have watched Lakey work on spiritual energy paintings and I know he does not look at the photos. I felt certain he had painted this using only the spiritual energy of the baseball card.

Cheryl didn't pick up Jason's painting when it came in. She wanted to wait for her mother and the rest of her family to get to Ventura so they could pick it up together. She asked us to display it in our gallery in the meantime.

One evening a customer had a vision as she looked at Jason's painting. She saw the angel performing ballet. I thought she was imagining this, and told her that the painting had been commissioned using the spiritual energy of a baseball card. Nonetheless, the customer remained certain of her vision.

When Cheryl and her family came in to pick up the painting several weeks later, I told them about the woman's vision of a ballet angel.

Her aunt stared at me in amazement. "But Jason did practice ballet! His baseball coach recommended it to increase his agility. Jason enjoyed doing all the ballet moves and would show them to us for hours."

Patricia's 20 Angels

In the spring of 1996, two women came to the store to commission a painting with a photo of a very pretty young woman. Each time they looked at it they would sob and cover their faces. I assured them their painting would be a comfort.

About two months later it was completed and delivered. A single angel was depicted, but when the women examined it, they were surprised to find 20 hearts drawn on the back. Nineteen of the hearts were on the back side and one was actually painted on the frame. They began to weep.

"How did Lakey know about Patricia?" they asked. "She died last year of cancer. She was 19 years old when she was diagnosed, and 20 when she died."

The women returned to our store in the fall of 1996 to tell us about some new insights. They now knew the angel in the painting was not ascending, but descending. They felt Patricia had returned to earth to comfort them in their time of grief.

Bubbles of Love

We met Debra in the winter of 1996. She comes from a home filled with abuse and co-dependence. She told us her most recent boyfriend had hissed at her like a snake. He was physically abusive, ran up large credit card debts, and stole everything of value she owned before leaving her for another woman.

Debra commissioned a spiritual energy painting using a photocopy of her driver's license. The painting that came back had two angels hand in hand and was filled with circles.

Both Debra and I were baffled. What could it mean? When Andy Lakey made a personal appearance at our store in April 1996, Debra brought her painting in.

"What do these circles mean?" she asked him.

"I have never felt such need for bubbles from any other photo I received. But I knew you needed bubbles of love," he responded.

"What do you mean by bubbles of love?" she asked.

"There's a lot of negativity in the universe," Lakey replied. "Whenever I feel someone needs protection from this energy, I visualize them surrounded by bubbles of love and protection. The energy of your photo told me you needed this protection."

Debra feels the two angels symbolize the bond she has with her mother. This bond has been strengthened since she's had her painting. Debra's life has taken some positive turns. She visits our store every few months and tells us about the good things that continue to happen.

Most recently a fellow worker who had been harassing her for over a year changed his entire attitude. He and Debra have become friends. Debra still has a long way to go but now she has her bubbles of love to protect her.

An Angel for Kevin

Twenty-seven-year-old Kevin was working as a professional scuba diver when he was killed by an underwater avalanche off the coast of New Orleans on Thanksgiving Day 1996. Kevin's mother Judy and stepfather Carl were devastated by this tragedy, and Carl lost 50 pounds after Kevin's death.

On March 10, 1997, Carl came to our store with an urgent request. He had a photo of Kevin and wanted Lakey to use it to paint a 7-by-7-inch spiritual energy painting for Judy. He needed the painting by March 17, which he told us was Kevin's birthday. Carl said he planned to visit Judy that day in North Carolina.

It was unusual for Lakey to complete a painting in less than six weeks, but Carl said he needed it in ten days. I called Lakey and explained the situation. Considering the circumstances, Lakey said he would try to make the short deadline.

The painting arrived via express mail on the morning of March 17. Carl came by to pick it up.

It was one of Lakey's beautiful diamond-shaped angel portraits. It had one angel traveling up three rays of light.

"Do you see anything in this painting about Kevin?" I asked.

After thinking for a moment he said, "No, but I got this painting for my wife. I'm taking it to her this afternoon. Maybe she'll know what it means."

Several months later Judy came by the store and told us how much she liked the Lakey painting.

"Carl was not totally truthful with you," she told us. "March 17 was not Kevin's birthday. He wanted the painting by that date so he could bring it with him when he visited. Our marriage had fallen apart after Kevin's death, and Carl thought the painting might bring us back together again.

"After leaving your store," she went on, "Carl walked four blocks to the beach. There he sat on a bench with the angel painting on his lap. He looked at the ocean and saw the sky was clear and bright blue. Then Carl saw something that still brings tears to his eyes. On the horizon sat one lone white cloud. The cloud was shaped exactly like an angel."

Carl, who in the past prided himself on being scientific and non-religious, had found some spirituality. He is certain that the cloud was a sign from Kevin that everything was going to be all right.

Carl and Judy have used their newfound spiritual bond to heal their marriage. When they returned from a recent trip to Holland, Judy brought Francesca a beautiful blue Dutch angel. This, Judy says, is for all her help in saving their marriage.

Jessie's Star

In the spring of 1997, Mary-Pat, a woman in her mid thirties with long, wavy, honey-blond hair and bright blue eyes, purchased a spiritual energy painting in honor of her friend Jessie. Mary-Pat and Jessie used to ride horses together. In 1991, Jessie committed suicide by driving his car into a tree.

Mary-Pat gave us the program from Jessie's funeral and asked that Lakey use it to create a 10-inch star-shaped painting. Jessie's star was completed in record time (less than three weeks). Lakey said he felt this painting was needed right away.

When she saw the star, Mary-Pat cried. She took it home, cradling it as if it were a child. We could see it meant a lot to her. The next morning she returned, visibly shaken.

"Something very intense happened last night," she reported, and then began sobbing.

"I went home after work and switched on the light. As I did, there was a blue flash and everything went dark. No other lights in the house would turn on. I held Jessie's star in my hands and ran my fingers over it as I sat in the dark. I felt something unusual at the top of the star. It was like a broken triangle shape. I had no idea what it was.

"As I found my way through my apartment," she continued, crying, "I eventually managed to get one light turned on. With the light on, I looked at the painting more closely. The pattern appeared to be a broken wishbone. A gold cord linked the small end of the wishbone to the angel on Jessie's star. I called Jessie's former fiancee, Wendy, and asked if there was any significance attached to a wishbone in Jessie's life. Wendy said, 'Only Jessie and I knew about this! We would always save the wishbones when we ate chicken or turkey. We would let them dry and break them. Our last meal together was Thanksgiving Day 1990 and we saved the wishbone from our turkey. We broke up shortly after that, and I threw the wishbone away.'

"On December 31 of that year Jessie committed suicide."

After speaking to Wendy, Mary-Pat realized the star was meant for Wendy. She brought the star back to the store the next morning, called Wendy, and asked her to pick it up. Wendy and her mother came in and when they saw Jessie's star they broke into tears. They were especially moved by the broken wishbone linked to the angel.

"Jessie lived a really sad life," Wendy told us, "and met a violent end. It's fitting that in his painting, his angel got the small end of the wishbone."

~ ~ ~

James Redfield's Angel Painting

In October 1996, I met James Redfield, author of the best-selling books, *The Celestine Prophecy* and *The Tenth Insight*. Redfield also wrote the introduction to Andy Lakey's first book, *Andy Lakey: Art, Angels and Miracles*. Redfield's painting by Lakey is 28 by 30 inches, predominately black and blue with eight angels moving toward eight rays of light. It is reproduced on page eight of *Art, Angels and Miracles.*

I asked Redfield about his painting.

"Last year Andy Lakey gave my wife Salle and me our beautiful painting. The moment we hung it on our living room wall, a new and powerful energy came into our home. We were amazed to see that our picture windows had fogged up and the form of a heart appeared on them. Inside the heart a multitude of colors began to shine. After several minutes the heart and its colors faded away. We have not seen anything like this in our home before or since."

Redfield finds Lakey's art deeply moving; it stimulates a newfound sense of possibility and wonder. In *The Tenth Insight* Redfield wrote about an angelic force similar to that experienced by Lakey.

Redfield's next book will further explore the meaning and function of Lakey's angels in relation to *The Celestine Prophecy* insights.

Chapter Five

A Psychomanteum in the Gallery

In the spring of 1996 we completed our art gallery at *Things from Heaven.* Shortly after opening our new space many strange and unexplainable things began to occur. The most disturbing of our experiences was when customers reported that they were receiving full color 3-dimensional messages from the other side.

I wondered if our customers were being given some sort of a psychological cue that was causing them to hallucinate. Or maybe we were attracting people with mental illnesses to our store. The more these strange phenomena happened the more confused and afraid my wife and I became.

As I analyzed the stories, I found there was no distinct category I could use to determine who would experience the phenomena in our gallery. People of all ages, races, religions and cultural backgrounds saw literally the same kinds of things. The more I saw and the more stories I recorded, the more I believed that a portal to the other side existed in the back of our store.

I had never heard of anything like this happening. I assumed this was the only place of its type in the world. I was cautious not to publicize what was occurring in fear that we might face public ridicule or even religious persecution.

One day in the summer of 1996, a customer named George came into our store to visit our Andy Lakey Gallery. George is a collector of Andy Lakey's art and I had shared several of our stories about the unusual occurrences happening around Lakey's works with him. That day George brought a book for me, *Reunions* by Dr. Raymond A. Moody.

George said, "Keith you have to read this book to know what's happening in your gallery. What you're experiencing is not a local phenomena. Read this and you'll understand."

People are always giving me one book or another that they feel I need to read. I usually take their books, put them down somewhere and forget about them. For some reason, however, I felt I had to read the book George had given me.

That night I took the book home and read it in one sitting. I was amazed by the synchronicity between Dr. Moody's work and my own. The book told of Dr. Moody's thirty year quest to study and build Psychomanteums. The ancient Oracle of the Dead in Greece was civilization's first Psychomanteum. It consisted of a series of mazes leading to a room illuminated by flickering lights with a polished metal cauldron as its focal point. This and other sacred sites throughout the world influenced Dr. Moody in his construction of modern-day Psychomanteums.

Dr. Moody is best known for his work of bringing scientific validation to near death experiences. His book, *Life After Life*, is now the handbook for near death experience study. Dr. Moody's more recent work in constructing Psychomanteums has created a new concept in grief centers. Here people are allowed to handle grief in a more direct way. The Psychomanteum allows them to avoid psychological counseling and go directly to their loved ones and discuss their grief first hand.

Dr. Moody's Psychomanteums consist of a dimly lit room with a comfortable chair that faces a raised mirror. Those entering this room often see images of deceased loved ones and receive reassuring messages from the other side.

Moody's book, *Reunions*, also discusses the use of art to induce an altered state. He quotes scientific studies that document the profound spiritual experiences people have had when coming into contact with great works of art.

It wasn't my plan to build a Psychomanteum at our store. I feel, however, that we were directed by God to build a grief center similar to those constructed by Dr. Moody. We use Andy Lakey's art instead of mirrors or pools of water to allow our customers to glimpse the other side. Our center continually helps people in dire grief find renewed faith, hope and spirituality.

A New Path For Sundance

In late summer of 1996, a Native American man who called himself Sundance came into our store. A large man with strong features, he was dressed shabbily and clearly had not bathed in weeks.

Sundance was upset and looked disdainfully at my son Keith, who was at the counter. "To have a store like this," Sundance said, "You have to believe in God, don't you?

"Yes, you do," replied Keith.

"Well, I don't. I don't believe in anything any more!" Sundance said.

Keith called to his mother, and Francesca, being the

caring person she is, took the time to hear him out.

"There is no God!" he said. "If there was a God, he wouldn't have treated me the way he has."

"What do you mean ?" Francesca asked.

"Two years ago I was happy. I had a good job, a wife and two young sons. We lived on the Apache Reservation in Arizona. One day we were driving in our car and a drunk driver hit us head-on. My wife and sons were killed.

"After this happened, I gave up. I left the reservation and got involved in alcohol and drugs and crime and violence. I didn't care about anyone. I've drifted from city to city. I have lived on the streets of Ventura for the past six months. My life is worthless. There's nothing anyone can do for me."

"You have to pray to God about your situation," Francesca said. "You know, God loves you. Come and see our art gallery. It's very spiritual and I think it will help you."

He reluctantly agreed, and when he entered, his mouth dropped. "I recognize these angels. They're the angels of my people," he said.

Francesca told Sundance to find a painting that he felt called to him, put his hand over it, and pray about his wife and children. He found a painting with one golden angel, placed his hand over the angel, closed his eyes, gasped, and seemed entranced. After five minutes of not moving, tears poured from his eyes.

"I've been wrong," he cried. "So wrong about everything. I saw my wife. She said not to worry about her. She was happy where she was. She told me I should find another woman to marry.

"Then I saw one of my sons. He told me he would always love me. He also said not to worry about him because he too is happy.

"Then I saw God, who told me I'm on the wrong path. I need to return to my reservation and work with orphaned Indian children. I'm going back. I'm going to tell all the Apache people to come to your store and find the spirituality you allowed me to find."

The next day Sundance returned, bringing Francesca a crystal. "This crystal represents the power of the universe," he said. "Use it to keep the power of God in your store."

He returned again the next day with a Native American herb called sweet grass. "This herb should be burned in your store every day to cleanse any negativism that might be here."

The third day Sundance returned with a member of the Hell's Angels motorcycle club. He brought Francesca a brass bracelet, said a final farewell and left on the back of a Harley. He has never returned.

Ashley's Birthday Wish

In August 1996, a mother, daughter and grandmother came into our store. They were looking for pictures of angels to have engraved on a memorial plaque for Kathy, the grandmother's daughter, the mother's sister, the little girl's aunt. Kathy had died in May. They found what they wanted on some of our angel stickers.

While perusing gift items, the mother came upon the shrine at the back of the store. She wrote an intercession that read: "God, please hold my sister Kathy in your wings until she grows wings of her own."

As they came to the counter to pay for their goods, eight-year-old Ashley said she also wanted to write an intercession to God.

She got a piece of paper from the shrine and wrote: "God, Lord. Please don't let Kathy slip through your hands like she did mine."

"Would you go with me to put my intercession on the shrine?" Ashley asked her mother.

"Can't you see I'm busy buying things?" the mother responded.

"Don't worry, Ashley. I'll go with you," Francesca said.

I totaled up the ladies' order while Francesca and Ashley walked to the other end of the store to leave her intercession on the shrine. Ashley was very emotional, and began to sob openly. Francesca guided the little girl into the art gallery to comfort her. She suggested Ashley find a painting that she felt had her Aunt Kathy in it. Ashley placed her left hand over a small painting of four pink angels. Francesca told Ashley to close her eyes and say a prayer to God about her aunt.

Ashley appeared to go into a trance and made a soft gasping sound. After about four or five minutes she recovered a bit. She began to cry three long teardrops from each eye, and seemed as if she was mesmerized.

"I saw Aunt Kathy and she said 'Happy birthday'" Ashley said over and over.

Skeptical as I had been about these phenomena up to this point, I knew something had really happened this time. I didn't think an eight-year-old girl could make this up. She was crying too hard for this to be a childish prank.

I asked Ashley's mother if we could have her name,

address and phone number so we could verify this event. She agreed. After Ashley had calmed down, I asked if she could recall what happened. I carefully wrote down every word she said.

"The first thing I saw was clouds. Then the clouds opened up and I saw beautiful golden gates. The gates opened and then I saw God."

I interrupted at this point and asked Ashley, "What did God look like?"

"God was beautiful," she said. "He had long brown hair and a brown beard. And he wore a long white gown that glistened.

"I said 'God, I want to see my Aunt Kathy. I want to see her right now!' God said, 'Ashley, what you're asking me to do is against the rules. We don't do things like this here.'

"Then he said, 'Ashley, you're such a good little girl, and I'm a very nice man, so I'm going to break the rules today. You can see your Aunt Kathy for one minute.'"

Ashley then said, "My Aunt Kathy came to me. She was floating toward me on a cloud. She said, 'Ashley, I love you and I'm always going to love you. Don't worry about me. I'm happy here in Heaven.' Then she said, 'Happy birthday, Ashley. I always loved your birthdays.'"

Ashley explained that her Aunt Kathy came close to her, held her hand and softly said, "Ashley, there's something I want you always to remember. Never, never give up your dreams."

"After that," Ashley said, "Aunt Kathy told me she had to go back to God. I saw her float away and the golden gates close. Then I came back."

Tina's Heavenly Vision

Twelve-year-old Tina is a child actress who has appeared in many films, including starring roles in several major Hollywood films. She came into our store in the spring of 1995. Her mother is a friend of one of our regular customers.

Francesca showed Tina the art gallery and she immediately fell in love with Andy Lakey's art. She found a numbered sketch and purchased it.

"Before you go," Francesca said, "run your hands over Lakey's paintings so you can feel their energy."

Tina was particularly captivated by a painting Lakey had created using the spiritual energy of Our Lady of Guadalupe. Francesca told Tina to put her left hand over the painting, close her eyes and say a prayer. Tina did this, then went into what was becoming a familiar trance among our gallery-goers.

After five speechless minutes, her first word was "Awesome!"

"You won't believe what I just saw!" Tina said to her mother.

"What did you see?" her mother asked.

"I saw your best friend Linda who died last year. She told me to tell you not to worry about her," Tina said. "She's happy where she is. She also wanted me to tell you thank you for the beautiful plaque you placed on the pier for her."

Her mother began to cry.

"Tina," she said, "You couldn't have known anything about that. After Linda passed away last year, she was cremated. We went out on a pier and scattered her ashes over the ocean. Later we had a memorial plaque made and we mounted it at the end of the pier."

Neither Tina nor her mother could explain what had occurred. Francesca and I both knew they received a message from the other side.

Police Officer Michael Clark

In the fall of 1995, Police officer Michael Clark of Simi Valley, California was shot and killed in the line of duty.

He was the first officer killed in action in the history of the Simi Valley police force. He left behind a wife and five-month-old son.

About a year later, Officer Clark's widow Jennifer came to our store. Francesca showed her into our gallery to see Lakey's paintings. Initially, Jennifer was skeptical. She said she couldn't feel anything coming from the paintings.

"Close your eyes and put your hands above a painting that calls you," suggested Francesca, "and say a prayer to God."

Jennifer noticed a pyramid-shaped painting of three large angels. She put her hands above two of the angels, closed her eyes and prayed. Suddenly, she drew in a quick breath and stared at the painting, seemingly entranced for several minutes. Then she shook her head and began to cry hysterically.

"This is weird. This is so very weird," she kept repeating.

"What is?" Francesca inquired.

For several moments Jennifer couldn't answer.

"I saw my husband," she said finally. "I always wondered what happened to him after he was shot. I also wondered how he would feel about my having another man in my life. But Michael said, 'I'm happy here. You don't have to worry about me. You need to go on with your life.' Michael also said it was all right for me to have another man in my life to love."

Jennifer left that day confused and frightened. Several months later, in April of 1997, she returned and wrote the following statement.

"In September 1996, I came to *Things from Heaven*. I put my hand on a painting by Andy Lakey. I immediately felt peace about my husband's murder. My husband Michael came to me and made me know that everything was going to be okay. I felt that Michael was really at peace and in a better place. It's been almost two years since his murder and I know now, since feeling the strength from Andy Lakey's painting, that everything is going to be okay."

Libby's Brother's message

In February 1997, an obviously poor couple and their eight-year-old daughter Libby came to our store. They quickly walked past the front area into the gallery, giving me the impression they knew what they wanted. Only later did I find out they knew nothing about Lakey's art, or that we sold it. They were captivated by what they saw.

"Have you heard of Andy Lakey?" I asked.

They looked at each other questioningly, and then back at me, and together they responded "No."

"Maybe you've seen him on television. He's been on lots of shows."

They looked at me blankly.

"We don't watch television," the father said.

I told them about the many newspaper and magazine articles written about Andy Lakey.

"We don't read newspapers or magazines," the father said as he shook his head.

They apparently had no knowledge of Andy Lakey whatsoever. Ever the trained scientist, I decided they'd make a perfect control group. Having no expectations, they could validate or refute the strange phenomena we had been witnessing.

"There is something I'd like you to try for me," I said. "I'd like you all to close your eyes and run your hands about an inch above any painting on the wall that you feel calls to you personally."

They looked at me skeptically, and just to appease me, they each chose a painting and placed their hands near it. Both the husband and wife were amazed by what they felt.

"There's tingling and warmth. There's something about this art that brings peace and tranquillity."

They tried every painting and sketch on the wall and to their surprise, felt the same thing emanating from all of Lakey's art.

Libby suddenly spoke up. "I just saw my little brother!"

I looked around but saw no one.

"Is your little brother lost?" I asked.

"Libby's little brother died last year of a terminal illness," her father told me.

"My little brother spoke to me through the painting over there," Libby insisted. "He said he loved me and not to worry about him. He's happy where he is. We need to go on with our lives."

I told them things like this had happened several times before. I related some of the other incidents, and explained the Psychomanteum effect encountered by Dr. Raymond Moody. They concluded the heat and tingling they had felt was actually a portal connecting them to another dimension.

Mark and Scotty are Together Again

Claudia first came to our store in February 1997. Clearly

distraught, she looked around for a few moments before approaching Francesca.

Claudia cried as she poured out her life's tragedies. Her son Mark had been killed in a street gang related incident in October 1996. Her father had died of a terminal illness three months later. Four other relatives had also died in the past six months. She wondered why she had to live her life hurting the way she did.

Francesca told her about other customers who had come to the gallery grief-stricken and that many had been helped by the power of prayer and the angel art.

"Have you gone into the room at the back of the store?" Francesca asked.

"No, I only glanced in. What's in there?"

"We have a major collection of art by angel artist Andy Lakey."

"Who's he?" Claudia asked.

As they walked back, Francesca briefly told Claudia how Lakey's near-death experience changed his life, and explained that to truly experience the art, you had to run your hands over it.

Francesca directed Claudia to find a painting that she felt called to her personally, put her hands over it, close her eyes and pray. She told Claudia she would pray with her.

Reluctant and afraid, she nevertheless did as Francesca suggested. After a few moments, tears began to roll down her cheeks. Her emotions seemed out of control as she reported her vivid experience.

Claudia saw two figures. One was her son Mark and the other was her father Scotty. Mark was sitting down and Scotty was standing behind Mark with his hand on his shoulder. They told her they were okay. They were together. Claudia felt a comforting presence.

After leaving the store, Claudia repeatedly saw the picture of her son and father flash into her mind. It continued to haunt her.

A few months later Claudia awoke from a sound sleep with an overwhelming compulsion to put the images she had seen in the painting on paper. She made a pencil drawing and a few weeks later felt compelled to paint what she had drawn.

For days Claudia cared about nothing but completing the painting of her vision. Her family became concerned. She did not know why she had to paint the picture; she just knew she had to do it.

When the painting was completed, Claudia reported that she felt the presence of angels all around her, and throughout the world as well. Lakey's art has touched her life forever and the healing vision continues to give her strength and hope to carry on.

There's a Hole in the Gallery

We were closing the store one evening in the fall of 1996 when Katherine and Gayle dropped by. Both are respected members of our community. Katherine is the director of a local hospice and Gayle is a grief counselor who works with the terminally ill.

We had made the curious discovery that Lakey's paintings become active in the dark, and since the sun had just set, we decided to show them into the gallery. Francesca and I were both a bit anxious about how these respectable, conservative ladies would react to such an offer, and relieved when they accepted enthusiastically.

We instructed them to run their hands just above the paintings. At first both reported feeling a general sense of love and peace. Then suddenly Gayle asked Katherine, "Did you see what I saw?"

"No," Katherine responded. "What did you see?"

"An angel, as tall as you, standing right in front of you."

Katherine was shaken, but did not see anything. Then,

she told us later, as she looked directly into a painting, it began to disappear. A portal seemed to open up in the solid wall and expanded outward until half the gallery wall opened into a long tunnel. She felt that she could pass right through the portal, as if a doorway to another place had opened.

"My God, the wall is disappearing," she said.

Gayle grabbed her arm and sharply tugged her.

"Stay in your body, Katherine," Gayle said. As she spoke, the portal closed and disappeared. Katherine was sadly disappointed.

All four of us then witnessed a light show emanating from the paintings as they glowed and pulsated in the darkness. We could all see energy in waves of white, green and blue.

Katherine and Gayle stayed with us for a long time that evening. We discussed what had happened and eventually concluded that the portal had not really closed at all. The opening to the other side is ever present.

Katherine felt she had experienced a new dimension of God, His angels and our immortal souls, and this incident enabled us to open our minds to the possibility of the peace, love and hope this other dimension holds.

Chapter Six

Miraculous Healings

People have experienced healings from Andy Lakey's paintings ever since we hung them in our store. At first we saw people overcome back pain and fatigue. As time went on, we were amazed by documented cases of the paintings curing everything from heart conditions to AIDS. The following are some of the most amazing healings we have seen so far.

The Gift

Shortly before Christmas in 1995, Diane and Richard visited our store. They loved the angel art, but a purchase was beyond their financial means. After some discussion, Richard told Diane he would buy her the videotape *A Touch of Lakey*.

Later that day, Richard returned to the store alone. Because his wife so loved the art, he had decided to splurge and buy her a 5-by-7-inch painting to surprise her with on Christmas morning.

Diane came in the week after Christmas to tell us how much her painting meant to her.

"I awoke Christmas morning, anxious to open my husband's gift of the videotape about Lakey's art. Things weren't going well for me that day. Richard's family was coming over for Christmas lunch, and my chronic arthritis combined with a dislocated shoulder were killing me. I couldn't raise my arms over my head. I hurt all over.

"Richard brought me my present. I hugged him and thanked him for the tape. Then he said, 'You really can't appreciate the tape without this gift.' To my surprise it was an original Lakey painting. I started to cry. It was the most beautiful gift I've ever received.

"I took my painting into the bedroom, ran my hand above it, and prayed to God for healing. A distinct coolness began seeping into my fingers, then up my arms and into my shoulders. I went into the kitchen to try and prepare the Christmas meal for Richard's family. As I picked up a pot, I realized a miracle had happened. All the pain from my arthritis was gone. And more than that, I could raise my arms over my head."

She then demonstrated her newfound agility.

~ ~ ~

Diane has come to our store many times since then. She tells us that her pain has never returned.

The Golden Angel

Toni first came to *Things from Heaven* in the fall of 1995. She was scared, homeless and desperate, and she felt as if some force had guided her into the store. She didn't know why since she had no money and couldn't buy anything; she just felt that she had to come in.

She had just left her abusive husband and driven from their home in Northern California to Ventura. She and her two daughters were living in their car. She didn't know what they were going to do.

I told Toni about some local community resources that might prove useful. During our conversation, I mentioned the angel paintings. Francesca suggested she run her hands over them to see whether she could feel the energy.

Toni found a 6-by-8-inch painting depicting one solid golden angel and five rays of light. She closed her eyes and said a prayer to God, then placed her left hand about an inch above it.

"Ouch!" she screamed. "This painting just zapped me!"

"Look at her hand!" Francesca exclaimed. "There's a

red spot on it!"

I saw that there was indeed a red spot on her hand, and it faded away before my eyes.

Toni left the store but called back later that evening. "You're not going to believe this, but after I left I applied for a job. Well, they just called and arranged an interview for tomorrow afternoon."

The next afternoon before her interview, Toni stopped by and ran her hand over the golden angel. The red spot appeared again.

That evening Toni called again. "Can you believe this? I got the job!" She had also met a benevolent man who agreed to sublet part of his home to her and her children at a very fair price.

She has come to our store many times since. She eventually secured an even better job and became engaged to the gentleman whose home she was subletting.

Angels of Healing

Patricia scrimped and saved to purchase her 5-by-7-inch Lakey painting.

"I just knew I had to have it," she said. "It really means something to me."

In October 1996, her father was hospitalized with

congenital heart disease after becoming bloated and in constant pain. The doctors said he had fluid on his kidneys and liver. After a few weeks he was released, but his condition was terminal. Further hospital care was pointless, and it was decided it would be best for him to die at home.

Patricia placed her beloved painting at his bedside, hoping it would bring him some peace during his final days. That evening he was awakened by the sound of bells.

"It sounded like small glass bells ringing," he explained later.

Just then, the two angels in Patricia's painting left the canvas and, "transparent and glowing," proceeded to flutter around the room making the ringing noise. As he watched them in shock, he realized their ringing was a means of communication.

The first one said, "This poor man needs our help. He's in a lot of pain and it isn't his time to go yet."

"Let's see what we can do," the second angel replied.

He said that they then entered his body and he experienced a sense of warmth and peacefulness. He could still hear them talking.

The first angel said, "This man has so much water in

him he's rusting."

"His kidneys need the most work," the other one said. "Let's work on these now and come back later to fix his liver."

The next morning he awoke rested and alert. For the first time in many months, he was not bloated and most astonishingly, he had no pain. The next day he and Patricia came to our store and told me this story. He insisted I touch his stomach to prove he had no bloating or pain.

He has fully recovered, mystifying his doctors. He, on the other hand, is not at all amazed. He simply says God sent angels to save him.

~ ~ ~

I'd always had trouble with this story. I felt it was a little far fetched and lacked the ability to be confirmed by any scientific method. I decided to put it in my book only because it was interesting and thought provoking.

Later, however, in the summer of 1997, Margaret, a tall, slender woman in her mid-fifties came into our store and walked straight through, into Andy Lakey's art gallery.

I asked her about her knowledge of Lakey's art and she said, "I know about this art. I was in a couple of weeks ago and bought his book, *Andy Lakey: Art, Angels and Miracles*. I gave the book to a friend of mine named Janet. Janet had been to the hospital for cancer surgery. When they opened her up, they found the cancer was so advanced that there was nothing they could do for her. They sewed her up and sent her home."

Margaret continued, "Janet went home to die. The doctors gave her no hope. I thought Andy Lakey's book would give her some comfort."

Shortly after Janet read Lakey's book, Margaret said something strange and miraculous occurred. She told me the following story.

"Janet was awakened in the middle of the night by the sound of glass bells. As she looked into the darkness of her bedroom she was surprised to see two glowing beings of light like those in Andy Lakey's book. Then she heard the two figures speaking to each other. One said, 'This poor woman is suffering so much and it's not her time to die.' The other replied, 'Then let's do something about this.'

"The two angelic figures then entered Janet's body. As they did, she felt a distinct sense of peace. Ever since that night Janet has begun to feel better and make progress in her fight against cancer. Her doctors are amazed. They say it is nothing short of a miracle."

At this point I interrupted, saying in astonishment, "I've heard this story before."

Margaret replied, "Oh, Janet's probably been in and told it to you, hasn't she?"

"No." I replied, "I heard a story just like it from someone else—a man who came in several months ago. I really didn't believe his story then, but I think I do now."

A Star for Baby Ashley

In December 1996, the parents and grandparents of a baby named Ashley came to the store. She had been born two months premature on December 12, the day of Our Lady of Guadalupe's vision and miracle. Ashley was in grave condition and they needed a miracle. She weighed a little over two pounds and was surviving with the aid of two life-support systems.

Ashley was her parents' first child and her grandparents' first grandchild. The distraught family wrote notes and placed them on the shrine at the back of the store, then walked into the gallery. I told them Andy Lakey's story, and about the divine intervention that saved his life. They purchased a 5-by-7-inch painting to put next to Ashley's incubator at the hospital.

Two months later Ashley's family returned. Their

mood was much more upbeat. Ashley had surprised everyone and survived. She was coming home that week.

The grandparents commissioned a 5-inch star-shaped angel painting. They gave us two photos; one of Ashley hooked up to two life-support machines, and another more recent one of her in improved health.

We took both photos to Andy and told him about Ashley's miraculous recovery and the part his art had played in it. He asked me to make sure Ashley's story was included in this book.

Barbara - "It's Going to be okay."

Barbara came to our store in November of 1996. Her father-in-law, a man she dearly loved, had died the day before. She was extremely depressed, had found our store by accident, and wandered in. A sales representative for a major gift company, she was amazed by the quantity of angel gift items we had in stock. But she didn't stop to look at them for too long; she seemed to be drawn to the gallery immediately.

She had never heard of Lakey but was intrigued by his art and his story. I had her run her hand over one of the paintings, and she was surprised by the energy she felt. In her grief, the feeling was actually a comfort to her.

A week later she returned with a photo of her fathe[illegible] in-law and commissioned a spiritual energy paintin[illegible] She told us she and her husband needed the painti[illegible] help them through their grief.

Six weeks later, Barbara took the c[illegible] painting home. Her husband was away on busi[illegible] She took the painting into her bedroom, placed it to [illegible] side and [illegible] her hand over it. She thought about her fathe[illegible] and began to cry. Then a cold shiver ran down Barbara[illegible] as she heard a soft reassuring voice. It sounded like [illegible] father-in-law's voice.

"You don't have to worry," he said. "Everything's going to be okay."

Barbara thought her husband must have come home and she called to him. When he didn't answer, she realized she was alone.

Since this experience Barbara has felt much more at ease about her loss. She found the painting so comforting that she also commissioned a 5-inch star painting and a 4-by-6-foot abstract painting. She tells me they have brought new spirituality and hope into her home.

Danny's Miracle

It was in February of 1997 that two of our regular customers arrived with their cousin, a frail looking young man named Danny. He was HIV positive and looked like he was in the final stages of disease.

Danny walked with a cane in one hand and an I.V. in his other arm. His cousins guided him into the art gallery, being careful to help him maintain his balance. They directed him to a 3-by-4-foot painting, and held him, one on each side, as he stood in front of it.

They told Danny to put his left hand over the painting and say a prayer.

"Tell God you want to be healed," they said.

Francesca and I watched this seemingly futile effort, and could not help but feel deep sympathy for Danny and his family. It seemed an impossible thing to hope for.

"No one has ever been cured of AIDS," I whispered to my wife.

"Danny is the sickest looking person I've ever seen in the store," she agreed. "I doubt he lives another month."

Three months later, in May of 1997, Danny and his cousins strolled in. Rather than looking like he was on the brink of death, he was healthy and active. He attributed his newfound health to his encounter with Lakey's art.

We asked Danny to write down what he thought had happened.

"I was diagnosed HIV positive in 1988. In January of 1997, my condition worsened. I contracted meningitis. My weight dropped from 175 pounds to 130 pounds in less than 30 days. Everyone thought I was going to die.

"Out of desperation, my cousins took me to your angel store. They wanted me to see an exhibit by artist Andy Lakey. My cousins had me put my hands over Andy Lakey's painting and say a prayer.

"Less than two months after this encounter, all my infections stabilized and my weight has climbed to a happy 195 pounds. All my doctors are dumbfounded. I am grateful to Andy Lakey for helping me open my heart to God so I could be healed."

Chapter Seven

Divine Guidance

Our experience with the art, angels and miracles of Andy Lakey has often run in cycles. Like an earthquake fault or volcano, things are dormant for awhile then suddenly the spiritual Richter Scale becomes active. A two-day period in November 1996 was one such eruption. Three individuals and one family experienced what could only be called extraordinary divine guidance in connection with Lakey's art.

A Message for Erik

As we were closing the store one evening, a husband, wife and their six-year-old came in. The father actually waited outside while the mother and son entered. They lingered not long in the gift section, but headed quickly for the back gallery.

Neither had heard of Lakey, so I briefly recounted his story. Then I asked the boy to run his hand above one of the paintings. He was bewildered by the energy he felt, and quickly ran outside to get his father.

His father came in and, running his hand over the paintings, also felt the energy. Father and son stood there, engrossed in moving their hands back and forth over the paintings.

I began chatting with the man as his son wandered around running his hands over all the paintings. After a few minutes a very surprised child came back and reported to us that "the painting over there just talked to me."

"I've heard of this happening before," I said. "What did the painting tell you?"

"The angel said 'Hello Erik. How are you this evening?'"

"Did it say anything else?" I asked.

"Yes," Erik answered. "It said 'I'm the angel that told a little boy in the hospital not to worry, that everything's going to be okay.'"

I suspected Erik was kidding me. We have a video of a twelve-year-old boy named Matthew Tash, who was a patient at the Jules Stein Eye Institute in Los Angeles. The video shows Matthew receiving a message from God as he sat next to a Lakey painting. The message was identical to what Erik had just said.

"You've been to our store before and seen the video haven't you?" I said.

"We've never been to your store before," his father said. "We're from Bakersfield [two hours away]. We didn't intend to come to this store tonight. We were just driving around and saw an empty parking spot out front. My wife felt compelled to come in here. I wouldn't even be in here if Erik hadn't come out and gotten me."

"How did Erik know about the message to Matthew Tash?" I asked.

"Maybe he saw it on television and he's experiencing some kind of subliminal flashback," the man suggested.

"The show Erik quoted from aired on *CNN News* four years ago. Erik would have been only two years old."

"I don't know then," he shrugged. "I'm sure there's some logical explanation out there."

I sure couldn't think of one.

Diana's Message From God

We had just opened for business the next morning when a distressed middle-aged woman named Diana came in. She passed right through to the gallery as I followed.

"Get me a chair," she requested. "The energy of this

room is too much for me. I feel like I'm going to faint."

I brought her a chair and she sat down, sobbing uncontrollably.

"I feel the spirit of the Lord in this room," Diana said. She explained that she belonged to a sect of the Pentecostal church and believed she was being 'slain in the spirit.' Many Pentecostals fall down and speak in tongues when they come in contact with Lakey's paintings.

Not particularly fond of being alone with hysterical people, I called Francesca for help. She stayed with Diana while I attended to customers out front. I was embarrassed by the sound of Diana's sobs as other customers entered. She had become more of a mental health concern than a person having a spiritual encounter.

After about ten minutes Francesca came out front. "Something really weird is happening," she said.

"Should I call 911?"

"No," Francesca replied. "It's not what you think."

"After you left the gallery Diana cried for a while," she continued. "When she was able to compose herself she said, 'I want to visit with Andy Lakey the next time he comes to your store. I need him to lay hands on me so I can be spiritually healed.'"

"I told her Andy Lakey doesn't do healing work, and

that if she wanted to be healed, she had to pray to God."

Francesca then took a painting from the wall and placed it in Diana's lap. It had been commissioned by a lay Pentecostal minister for her church's prayer room.

"You need to put your hand over the painting," Francesca told her. "Close your eyes and say a prayer about what you need."

"What I really need is a job," Diana said.

She closed her eyes and went deep into prayer, when suddenly her pager buzzed.

"That was quick," Francesca said. "You're getting a reply from God already."

"This is the phone number of the job I just applied for," she said as she stared at her pager quizzically. Using our phone, she dialed back the number.

"Yes, I can work full time," she replied to the person on the other end.

"Yes, I can start tomorrow .... Yes, that salary is acceptable." She put the phone down.

"I can't believe it. I got the job."

She sat in the chair stunned.

"This has been a miracle," she mumbled. "I've never had anything like this happen to me before."

Diana left smiling, and with a new perspective on

God, the power of prayer and her own spirituality.

What's a Pentecostal?—I'm a Methodist

Two hours passed without incident, then Nancy and her boyfriend came in. A 19-year-old with blond hair and blue eyes, she walked briskly to the rear gallery as her boyfriend followed. Upon entering, she went directly to a 3-by-4-foot painting of 12 angels. A strange expression came over her face.

"I don't know what's wrong with me," she said as she put one hand over her eyes. "I feel like I'm going to faint."

Her boyfriend held her up while I got a chair.

"My boyfriend and I were driving in downtown Ventura, when I had an overwhelming compulsion to stop my car and get out. The only place we could find to park was in front of your store. We have never been to your store before, but I felt we had to go in. Even though there were many beautiful things in the front, I felt compelled to come back here.

"As soon as I walked in, I started to feel like my soul was leaving my body. I've never felt this way before. I had a dream once that something like this happened to me," she continued. "But I've never felt this in real life."

After a few minutes, she asked, "Who painted these paintings anyway?"

"Andy Lakey," I replied.

"Never heard of him. Who is he anyway?"

I told them Lakey's story. They were most impressed. Nancy's behavior was very similar to that of Pentecostals who believe they have been what they term 'slain in the spirit' by the Holy Ghost. So I asked if she was a Pentecostal or a Charismatic.

"What's a Pentecostal or a Charismatic?" She gave me a strange look and said, "I'm a Methodist."

Jennifer's Story

About an hour after the young Methodist woman left, Jennifer walked in. I inquired whether she was okay, since she look dazed.

"You know, the strangest thing just happened to me," she said. "I felt compelled to go into the back room of your store. What do you have back there?"

"Paintings by the artist Andy Lakey," I replied. "Have you heard of him?"

"Yes, I have," she said. "But I never imagined that his art was right here in Ventura."

"What's happening to you isn't unusual." I told her.

"I'll bet I can tell you what you've just experienced."

"Sure. What do you think's been happening?"

"For some reason," I began, "You've been driving aimlessly around Ventura today. The only place you could find to park was in front of our store. Am I right so far?"

"Yes," she nodded in astonishment.

"Once you parked, you felt compelled to enter our store. Then you felt drawn to the art gallery in the back."

She was silent.

"You've never been here before, have you?" I added.

"How did you know all that," she stumbled over her words. "Are you a Psychic?"

"No," I replied. "It's just that the same thing has been happening all day long. "

Jennifer spent a fair amount of time with Andy Lakey's art that day. She purchased a miniature painting and a silver pendant.

She's now a regular customer, and tells us that her relationship with us and the art of Andy Lakey has changed her life.

A Pomona Police Officer's Wife

After Jennifer left, things were quiet for several hours until Margaret and her two children arrived. She had black hair, intense brown eyes and appeared to be in her early thirties. She dragged her children through the store toward the back. ''She must be acquainted with the store and have some interest in Lakey's art,'' I thought.

Once in the gallery, she looked at me questioningly.

"I have heard about this artist and his angel art, but I never thought I would see it in person," she said. "I'm amazed because I didn't even mean to come here."

She was from Pomona, a town several hours away, where her husband was a police officer. They had just had a terrible fight, so she loaded her children into the car and drove north.

"For some reason," she told me, "I felt I should exit the freeway in Ventura. We drove around town and the only place we could find to park was in front of your store."

I told her this was not uncommon; in fact it had happened several times already that day. Moreover, we were the only Lakey gallery between Pomona and Sacramento, a distance of 500 miles.

Margaret and her children studied the paintings for about half an hour. After some searching she decided upon a miniature and purchased it. She said she believed the whole experience was a message from God. She needed to return to Pomona and build a more spiritual relationship with her husband. The Lakey painting would be the cornerstone of this process.

About a month later we hosted a special event with Lakey in attendance. Margaret and her husband came and thanked me for my help. They were working on rebuilding their relationship and both felt that the painting played some role.

Theresa's Message

Theresa, a major collector of Lakey art, recently purchased a painting valued at $3,000. She showed up at the store on the Tuesday morning following all the unusual activity. The odd thing is that we are closed Tuesdays, and she knows that. Francesca and I only happened to be there because we had stopped by to attend to some loose ends.

"I know you folks close Tuesdays, but I felt compelled to come to the store," she said with some concern in her voice.

Since it takes her 45 minutes to make the trip, it was truly unlikely that she drove all the way knowing we would be closed.

"Two nights ago, your son Kevin showed me a

miniature [3 by 3 inch] painting numbered 888. I wanted to buy it but I didn't. That night I couldn't sleep thinking about that little painting. The next morning, I went to church and on the way home, I found myself crying for no reason. All day yesterday I could think of nothing but that little painting. I finally got up this morning and felt I simply had to drive over here."

The next day we brought in some new art and reconfigured the gallery. The strange activity ceased, and we haven't had an active period like that since.

<u>Chapter Eight</u>

Meaningful Coincidences

Since we opened the store in 1995, a psychic connection between Andy Lakey and ourselves has grown. There appear to be forces over which Andy, my wife, and I have no control. Something predestined seems to be happening, and it keeps building and building. Each time it increases we reach a new level of spirituality. Only God knows where this is going to take us in the end.

~ ~ ~

Numerous meaningful coincidences have occurred in the past two years. How we got Lakey's art, how we sold more of Lakey's art than anyone else and how our lives have been changed are all coincidences.

Lakey believes there is no such thing as coincidence. The more I see happening around us, the more I believe him.

~ ~ ~

Lost With Lakey in Santa Barbara

It was May 11, 1996, and Andy had just completed an exhausting weekend of personal appearance at our store. I agreed to drive him back to his Santa Barbara hotel 45 minutes away. Francesca and our son Kevin came along.

I had obtained directions from the hotel earlier in the day and believed they were in my pocket. As we reached the freeway exit ramps to Santa Barbara, I reached into my pocket to find I had the wrong paper. Embarrassed, I told Andy my mistake. He did not know how to get to the hotel either, so I tried to remember the directions I had received on the telephone.

They said the hotel was on Bath Street, but not to exit on Bath because it was a one-way street going the wrong direction. I was to get off on another street, the name of which I couldn't remember, and cut into Bath Street from there.

We passed Bath Street and I exited at the next street, Carrillo. I drove down Carrillo for quite a long way and decided that possibly Bath paralleled Carrillo. I turned right and drove several miles. Bath Street did not appear.

By this time I was hopelessly lost. We were in an unsafe neighborhood, I was a little scared, everything was closed, and it was getting dark. Andy suggested we find a telephone booth, call directory assistance, get the number of his hotel and then get directions. Between us we had just one quarter and I gave it to Andy. When he called directory assistance, he was given the wrong number.

I was embarrassed and very lost. I knew Andy must be exhausted, hungry and missing his wife and children, who were at the hotel we couldn't find. But he wasn't concerned. He was excited.

"Something amazing is happening," he said. "Don't be afraid. We're right where we're supposed to be. For some reason the universe has diverted us to this spot. There are no coincidences! Maybe we would have been in an accident or maybe there's a message we are supposed to receive. Anyway, when the time comes for us to get where we're supposed to be we'll get there."

I didn't believe that was true but I was relieved that he did. I headed west and eventually found State Street, which I was familiar with. I turned back to Carrillo. There I found a gas station and asked directions. Bath Street was just two blocks down. The street isn't marked coming into town, only going out of town.

When I got to Bath Street I made a right turn. Something didn't seem right. This was a residential area. There were houses and apartments and no sign of a hotel. As we traveled down the street something caught my eye. A little house at 1013 Bath Street had been converted into a Japanese restaurant called Sushi Teri House.

"That looks interesting," I said. "Who'd like to eat?"

We were all very hungry by this point and didn't know when we would find the hotel.

Andy, Francesca and Kevin said, "Yes! Let's stop."

There was a place to park just across the street. We went in and were seated. Our server spoke very little English. As Andy had spent part of his childhood in Japan, he speaks pretty good Japanese and he ordered for us.

Francesca looked at the server and said, "Don't I know you?"

Now what, I thought. Does she think she knows her from a past life?

"I know you too," the Japanese woman said in the best English she could muster. "My husband and I went to your wedding."

Francesca and the Japanese woman who owned the little restaurant with her husband, had graduated from a special program at Roosevelt High School in Los Angeles in 1974. The last time we had seen her was at our wedding on May 10, 1975—twenty-one years before, nearly to the day.

"What are the odds of this happening?" Andy observed. "One in a million, or one in ten million? I told you we were being diverted. I told you something was going to happen. There are no coincidences."

After dinner we bade goodbye to our long lost friends. We found the hotel four blocks away. Within a block, there was a freeway entrance. If we had gone down one more street on the freeway, we would have been right at Andy's hotel and none of the evening's coincidences would have occurred.

After this experience, I read Lakey's book, *Andy Lakey: Art, Angels and Miracles*. It includes what he calls his Seven Lessons.

Lesson Number Five, although obviously written long before our experience, described exactly what had happened.

"There are no coincidences," it begins. "Life is a wondrous, complex journey, full of opportunity and meaning. Yet every time something unusual happens, skeptics will say it's just a coincidence.

"I don't believe that. Everything that happens, happens for a reason. Every so-called coincidence is actually a message from the universe, a form of guidance, an opportunity to grow as a human being and take another step along the path.

"It's up to us to see the meaning and act on the opportunity. It's also up to us to create opportunities; to create situations where a life changing coincidence can occur."

Keith! What Are You Doing Here?

In November 1996, I received a call from the producers of *Caryl and Marilyn*, a nationally syndicated television show.

"Do you sell angel gifts at *Things from Heaven*?" they asked.

I explained to them what we sold. They invited me to appear on the program and asked me to bring along some samples. I mentioned the art, but they said not to bring any paintings because Andy Lakey was going to be on the program with me.

As he had been trying for months to get us some media attention, I assumed he had arranged to have our store featured. Just one month before that he had arranged for me to speak about his art on another nationally syndicated television program, *Strange Universe*.

On the day of the *Caryl and Marilyn* taping, I made the one-hour drive to Hollywood and, once at the studio, unpacked the boxes of angel gift items I'd brought along.

The prop people were helping me arrange them when Andy arrived.

"Thank you for arranging this television appearance for me. I truly appreciate your help," I said to him.

He looked puzzled.

"Keith," he said. "What are you doing here?"

"Didn't you arrange this?"

"No," he answered. "I thought I was doing this show with Dannion Brinkley."

"If you didn't arrange for me to be here," I said, very confused by this point, "who did?"

"I don't know," he replied.

We asked one of the show's producers why I had been chosen to be on the program.

He thought for a moment and then replied, "We were looking for a local angel store, so we went through the Beverly Hills phone book. You were the only one in it so we called you."

"Why is your store listed in Beverly Hills?" Andy asked.

I told him that when I was setting up my Yellow Pages advertising, the only phone book I felt inclined to run an ad in was Beverly Hills.

"I have always thought it was a really bad marketing

decision," I added. "Until now, no one has ever called me about that ad."

This Painting is Meant for Your Gallery!

In the summer of 1996, Francesca and I drove to Andy's studio in Murrieta about two and a half hours away to pick up some large canvases and discuss future plans.

"I have a painting that's supposed to be in your store," Andy said during the conversation. "There's something about its energy that makes me feel it's for you."

He unveiled a 3-by-4-foot painting in a pink frame with cut mirror pieces. In the center was a large copper colored angel with a heart in its chest area. Raised letters bore the signature "Lakey 93."

Andy explained to us that each year he would select several paintings from his collection to raise money for charity. He wanted to use the money from this painting to help an orphanage in Mexico. Andy's conditions for purchase were that we pay up front and display it. But we were not to sell it for one year. Although it was a striking work, I could not afford these conditions. To tie up so much capital in one painting would hurt our cash flow.

"I feel this painting's energy should be in your store," Andy shrugged off my concerns. "I don't know why, but I can't shake this feeling.

"I realize it's kind of a spur of the moment thing," he added, "and a major financial decision. Take a photo of the painting and look at it again in a couple of weeks. See if you might reconsider."

I agreed. When we returned home, I developed my film and two weeks later Andy called. He asked me to take out my photo and look at it.

"Keith, I'm giving you first choice for this painting because I feel its energy should be in your store," he said again.

"I appreciate your concern and the opportunity," I replied. "But as I told you before, we can't afford to tie up our store's cash flow on one painting."

"I understand your situation," Andy said. "I have another dealer who might be interested. I just wanted to give you guys first choice."

"Sell it to the other dealer."

And so he did.

Four months later an associate of Lakey's called. One of the dealers was having financial difficulties and had lost her gallery. She had a major piece of Lakey art she needed to sell. I asked her to describe it.

"It's 3 by 4 feet, mirrored, and has a raised signature,"

came the response.

"How much money does she want up front?"

"Nothing," she said. "The woman is willing to deal on straight consignment. All she wants is what she paid for it."

Agreeing to take it sight unseen, I drove to her house to pick it up. Her husband brought it out of the garage and took the wrappings off.

"That's the painting Andy Lakey showed me last summer!" I blurted out. "He said it was supposed to be in our store."

She looked at me and smiled.

"Andy's done a lot of paintings that look kind of like this," she reminded me. "He's done more than 1600 paintings for collections and galleries around the world."

I myself had sold to people from Scotland, Australia, and more than ten different states in the U.S.

"The chance of this being the same painting Andy showed you last summer is very slight. I'd say one in a million," she concluded.

I loaded up the painting, took it to the store and hung it on the gallery wall. When I got the photo out and compared it to the painting, my suspicions were confirmed. It was indeed the same painting Andy had shown us six months before. He had been right—there was something about the energy of that painting that brought it to our store.

Donald Ball - Our Friend on the Other Side

In November 1995, I met Don and his wife Brenda. They were immediately taken by the beauty and spirituality of Lakey's art. Over the next few months, they purchased seven paintings. Six of them were painted using the spiritual energy of photos Don and Brenda provided.

Don and I had a lot in common and shared the same sense of humor. Coincidentally, Don had drawn the technical specifications for the ship I had been stationed on in the U.S. Navy. We always had much to talk about and formed a friendship that developed well beyond the usual customer relationship.

Don was concerned about the look of our store and created a plan to upgrade nearly everything. He designed a storage system that enabled us to keep a large amount of goods in a very small space.

One thing that really drove Don crazy was the art gallery. According to him, the lights were arranged all wrong. He and I tore out the entire ceiling and eventually installed a satisfactory system.

Don and Brenda were very spiritual people, a fact Lakey's art seemed to enhance in both of them. Don dedicated an entire wall of his living room to angel art. He named all the paintings and wrote a short explanation of each. The names and descriptions were engraved on brass plaques and mounted on the frames he made for each work of art.

Don had a joking relationship with Andy. Both men enjoy a good practical joke and each would try to outdo the other.

Lakey called Don posing as a television reporter and asked Don about a painting he did not have. Don and Brenda called Lakey pretending they were from the I.R.S. Lakey then called Don and Brenda and told them their Lake Tahoe Condominium had blown off the mountain. They had a wonderful time kidding each other.

In November 1996, a desperate message was on my voice mail from Brenda Ball. Don had suffered a massive stroke and was in the intensive care unit of a local hospital. When Francesca and I visited he did not look good, but his prognosis was encouraging. The doctor said his temperature was normal and that he had no blockages in his blood vessels. He could make a full recovery.

The day after visiting Don in the hospital, I did a guest

appearance on the *Caryl and Marilyn* show with Andy. He asked me how Don was doing.

"Is he going to die?" Andy asked.

"They say his vital signs are all good," I told him. "But truthfully Don didn't look that good. I don't know if he's going to live or not."

The next morning I got the tragic message from Brenda. Don had died of heart failure at 3:00 a.m.

"Don was looking much better Monday evening," Brenda cried. "He was sitting up watching television and he seemed to be in good spirits. I had been at his side for nearly a week," she said, "and I was exhausted. He saw my condition and said 'Don't worry about me. Go home and get some rest.'"

Shortly after that the hospital called to tell her Don had died.

Francesca and I were shocked. It had all happened so fast. Don was such a big, strong, outgoing person, it was hard to believe he could die so suddenly. Then Brenda told me Don had arranged everything for his death six months before. It was as if on some level Don had received a message from God about his impending death.

Using Andy Lakey's paintings, he had built a spiritual shrine. He had engraved spiritual messages on plaques which he attached to each. And he had set up every detail of his funeral plans.

Don also helped set up our store so it would be more successful, and in so doing showed us new aspects of the paintings, literally in a different light. A loved one's passing is never easy, but Don had done everything possible to ease the pain.

Andy visited about a week later. As we were standing in the gallery, we spoke about Don and how all of us missed our fun-loving friend. Suddenly, the gallery lights Don had installed began to flash erratically. The one most out of control was one I had adjusted to shine on Andy. It flickered like a candle and no matter how I adjusted it, continued to flash. The light had never flashed this way before and it has not done so since.

Andy was not alarmed. He knew it was Don playing one of his jokes on us from the other side.

Chapter Nine

Cross Cultural Views

Being situated a block and a half east of the well-known San Buenaventura Mission, *Things from Heaven* gets tourists from around the world. This diverse group of people has given us the opportunity to hear sometimes fascinating cross-cultural analyses of Lakey's art.

In the spring of 1996, a Russian diplomat rumored to be instrumental in establishing peace talks between the United States and Russia came with his wife to our store. He had also been a leader in the movement to bring democracy to the Soviet Union.

They were impressed by the paintings and held their hands over them. They felt the energy right away and said they would like us to open a store in Moscow! This way their people could experience the angels and the magical art for themselves.

~ ~ ~

We see about five or six Japanese tourists each week, and about 90 percent of them report feeling energy flow from the paintings. They often ask whether there are batteries in the frames that generate the heat and tingling. I turn the paintings over and let them examine the inside of the frames.

One Japanese couple was so impressed they purchased a copy of the video *A Glimpse of Lakey* so they could take it home and explain to their family what they had seen and felt.

In September 1996, a prominent San Francisco psychologist visited our store at the request of the UPN television news program, *Strange Universe.* Her near-death experience while on a 1993 Himalayan trek had led her to write a book entitled *I Believe in Angels.*

She arrived at our store in the company of the Tibetan Sherpa guide who carried her to safety from a 16,000-foot peak. We showed him Lakey's art and suggested he experience it by running his hands over the paintings.

"Don't ask him to do this," the psychologist said. "This isn't part of his belief system. He's a Buddhist!"

We assured her there was only one God in the universe and that we all have the same angels. The Sherpa agreed. He wanted to know what he might feel from the paintings. As he moved his hands above the paintings, a smile crossed his face and he closed his eyes.

"These are the most sacred paintings I have ever seen," he said after a few moments. "When I run my hands over them I feel as if my soul is being drawn in."

We get about twenty or thirty European tourists in the store each week, mainly from Great Britain, the Netherlands, Germany and Scandinavia. They are often the most skeptical of all our customers. Few have ever seen or even heard of the idea of dedicating an entire store to angels. None had heard of Lakey.

The British and the Germans seem to be the most frequently rigid in their reactions. They often think we are joking about the energy people feel and they are too inhibited to run their hands over the paintings themselves.

Nevertheless, about eight out of ten do feel it, then try to rationalize what they feel. Often I have to take sketches out of their frames and hold them up in the air for their scrutiny. They are totally perplexed by the phenomena.

Chapter Ten

Religious Views

The spiritual impact of Lakey's art seems to have universal appeal and to cross all religious lines.

~ ~ ~

Roman Catholic

Roman Catholics as a group tend to be loyal followers of Lakey's work. As a painting hangs in the Pope's Vatican Collection in Rome, it is hard for devoted Catholics to dispute the spirituality of Lakey's endeavor. Despite this inarguable endorsement by their Church, some are still unconvinced.

In the fall of 1995, a Roman Catholic nun came in with a lay person. I explained that many people who hold their hands over the paintings feel an energy. The nun ran her hand over the painting and was startled by the heat and tingling.

"This is a trick," she reprimanded me sternly. "You just gave me a psychological cue that made me feel what I felt."

I assured her this was not a trick. I suggested we have her friend, who was at the other end of the store looking at jewelry, run her hand over the painting to prove my point.

"I don't want you to say a single word to my friend," she said. "I know you'll give her a subliminal cue. Let me speak to my friend in my own way."

When her friend entered the gallery, the nun turned to her and said, "Sometimes people get messages from God when they pass their hands over this painting. See if you get one."

The friend ran her hands over the painting for a few minutes with no success.

"Sister," she finally said, "I don't get a single message from this painting."

The nun looked at me and smiled. Then her friend continued.

"All I get is heat and tingling."

Pentecostal

Juanita Jones, a forceful black lay minister of the Pentecostal Church, first visited our store in the fall of 1995. She immediately questioned whether our store was truly in the hands of Jesus Christ or just a tool of the devil.

I sensed trouble.

"What do these represent?" Juanita demanded about the angel paintings.

"These are angels," I replied.

"They don't look like angels to me!" she announced.

I recounted how Lakey had seen beings of light during a near-death experience, how he received a message from God to paint 2,000 angel paintings to represent each year that had passed since the birth of Christ. She was unconvinced.

"Run your hands over the paintings and tell me what you feel," Francesca suggested to her.

Juanita hesitated. I cringed.

"Now we've done it," I thought to myself. "This woman is going to start yelling that our store is satanic or something."

As Juanita moved her hand an inch above one of the paintings, a peaceful expression came over her face.

"Glory Hallelujah," she shouted. "These paintings are anointed by the holy spirit."

Juanita quoted Isaiah 10:27 from the Old Testament, a Bible verse about the anointing of the yoke of the Lord. It says that if God gives you a task, and you do it well, it will be so blessed that it will radiate God's presence.

Since that day, Juanita has brought literally hundreds of people to our gallery. She comes in every few months and holds a Pentecostal service with her parishioners.

Her parishioners commissioned a special painting for their church. Seven angels are depicted therein, and they feel this represents their love of God. It has brought them a great deal of healing and spirituality.

Hindu

Our neighboring enterprise is a small market run by a traditional Indian family. Hindu symbols are placed prominently throughout the store and they are faithful to their religion.

Mike, the store's owner, came next door to visit us one day. Passing his hand over the paintings, he expressed his amazement at the energy each possessed.

As we were talking, an angry young woman came in. She was neatly dressed and full of defiance.

"I am a Christian and I don't believe in angel worship," she said. "How do you know these angels are the angels of God? These could be the fallen angels of Satan."

"I don't know what your religion teaches you," Mike said to her, "but mine teaches me that God is love. How can you find evil in something so beautiful as an angel?

Put your hands over these paintings and feel their power."

Eyeing him suspiciously, she refused.

"Lady, you have nothing to be afraid of," Mike assured her. "These paintings can't hurt you. Don't you know God don't make no bad angels?"

Chapter Eleven

What the Messages Have Taught Us

Every day we learn new lessons. Some are painful, others are beautiful. But all have meaning and purpose. Since opening our store in the spring of 1995, my family and I have traveled a great distance on the road to spirituality.

I am certain we will travel much farther and learn many more important lessons before our journey is through.

Here are the most important—and interesting lessons that dealing in angel art has brought our way.

1. There is Abundance in the Universe

Lakey gives away 30% of everything he earns. In general, it can be said that this is three times more than the most generous philanthropists in our society. He also requests that those of us who sell his art give away a minimum of

5% of our net earnings from his art to help others.

Early in 1996 he had a third vision from the angels. They directed him not to sell some sketches he had drawn at the Great Pyramid of Giza in 1995 but rather to give them away. He had been offered $2,000,000 for the sketches but he obeyed the angels. He began giving them away to those who purchased his other art. The condition of this gift was that the recipients had to promise to help children, either as a volunteer or a donor to a children's charity.

In December of 1996, while a guest on TV's *Caryl and Marilyn,* Lakey promised to make a gift of art to all young people aged eighteen or younger on the condition that they write a letter in their own handwriting promising not to take drugs, drink alcoholic beverages or use any tobacco products.

My wife and I visited Lakey's studio in the winter of 1997 and found it filled with cardboard tubes and boxes. The boxes overflowed with more than 8,000 letters from young people pledging not to use drugs, alcohol or tobacco. The tubes would be used to mail their art. Lakey had hired two people just to stuff the tubes with artwork. He was sending out about 250 pieces a week to meet the demand which would take at least eight months to complete. It was costing him thousands of dollars to fulfill his promise but he felt that if he helped just one young person, it would all be worthwhile.

Our association with Lakey has shown us how the more you give, the more you get. *Things from Heaven* donates to many Ventura County charities. Indeed it is our policy to never turn down a genuine charitable request.

"You're a start-up business," people have said to me. "How can you afford to give away so much of your income?"

How can we afford not to give back what God has so graciously provided us so that we may help those in need? Approximately 20% of our net profits go to help others. If we could, we would give more.

There is abundance in the universe. We know that and we give away more than money. When we first started out in business no one helped us. We had no background in retail sales, and didn't even know where to purchase angel items. We stumbled through a trial-and-error approach to build our business.

When we are approached by others starting retail businesses, we go out of our way to help them find the products and sources needed to be successful. I know an individual who charges as much as $50,000 for the same type of information. We prefer to provide ours free of charge.

There are those who say we are stupid for giving away trade sources. But we believe everything you give comes back ten-fold, and so far our beliefs have been affirmed and our generosity has been rewarded.

2. No One Really Dies

What Lakey saw in his 1986 vision changed his life and the lives of millions of other people as well.

Every day we see people cry as they touch Lakey's art, and we know there is more to life than doctors and scientists tell us. There is beauty, hope and a spirit of loving. No one ever really dies. Souls just take on new dimensions of growth and transformation.

Raymond Moody, M.D. has reviewed thousands of documented reports of near-death experiences. He found no differences in terms of time of day, age, religions or cultures. Moody developed a chamber called a *Psychomanteum* to help people address grief over lost loved ones. Many of Moody's patients receive messages of hope from the other side as they sit in this chamber. The messages are nearly always the same: "I love you. I'll always love you. Don't worry about me. I'm happy where I am.

Go on with your life. We'll be together again."

At *Things from Heaven* we regularly see people come in contact with the souls of lost loved ones as they pray over Lakey's paintings. The messages these people report are similar to those received by the grief-stricken at Dr. Moody's Psychomanteums. We were not biased by the evidence from Dr. Moody's centers, because we were unaware of Moody's work until sometime after similar phenomena began occurring at our store.

3. Fear is the Root of All Evil

Angel art is attacked by some people, particularly those with a somewhat narrow focus on spirituality. Some appear to have found a great deal of religion but very little love for others.

Members of seemingly cultish religious groups often visit our store, preoccupied with "the fear." Satan is always present for them and ready to trick them into falling into his clutches.

"You're worshipping angels," they tell us. "Don't you know angels are evil idols? Andy Lakey's art might represent fallen angels."

I have had to patiently stand by while mothers dragged their children from our store, calling us "devil worshippers."

We intend that there be only God's love in our store, and only God's love in Lakey's art. I hope to be able to convey this love to all visitors in a way they can understand.

Lakey's art, for me, reinforces the notion that we need to have love in our hearts. It gives people in need new hope; it reinforces the spirituality we all have, and it shows us there is more to life than meets the eye. God sends His angels to bring His love to the world and to dispel the fear.

4. Prayer is Powerful

When Lakey faced his death and cried out his plea to God from the floor of his shower, it was just the beginning of his personal transformation. God gave Lakey a second chance, and also challenged him to make good on his promise to help humankind.

Prayer is powerful. We tell people to be careful what they pray for, because they just might get it. People pray every day at our store. We have seen miraculous healings after people place their hands above Lakey's paintings and whisper their prayer.

One day in 1995, a very skeptical gentleman waited

while his wife shopped for angel gifts. He was clearly embarrassed and uneasy about being in the store. In an effort to make conversation, I asked him how he was. He said he had hurt his back that morning and had been in terrible pain all day.

I suggested that he pass his hand just above a painting and say a prayer about his pain. He looked at me as if I were crazy.

"What the heck," he finally shrugged. "I'm in so much pain now I'll try anything."

I led him to a painting, then told him to close his eyes and pray to God. He did so with no result. He did not feel any energy coming from the painting. Two other men came into the store and ran their hands above the painting as he watched. The others were astonished by the energy they felt. As they discussed their reactions with me, the other man interrupted.

"I just wanted to tell you my back pain just vanished. This is a miracle," he said

He left the store walking straight and with no pain.

5. We are All on Our Own Paths to God

Our experience has shown us there is no right or wrong religion. People of many religions from every corner of the earth have come to our store and had similar experiences. There is just one God and mankind has developed many ways to worship this God.

Roman Catholics are often possessive about Lakey's paintings. As the Pope has a painting, they consider it Roman Catholic art and wonder why anyone other than a Catholic would want to purchase the paintings.

Protestants have said, "Don't Catholics know Christ's love is the answer to all the world's problems? This is what Lakey's paintings are supposed to teach us."

Some Jewish customers tell me the paintings represent the angels to which their ancestors alluded in ancient texts. They explain that angels brought the Jews messages from God. They see Lakey's angels as a sign that God loves them and that with faith in God, miracles can happen.

I have heard Moslems claim angels play an important role in their religion because it was Archangel Gabriel who brought the Koran to Mohammed. They see Lakey's art as yet another way God is sending His truth to the world.

Hindus claim the paintings represent the angels of their faith since Hinduism is the world's oldest practiced religion. Unlike Christians, Hindus believe all God's angels have been sent to earth for the good of humankind. To them Lakey's paintings are all good and all holy.

Native American visitors have explained that the paintings represent their God's messengers; they are a sign that all religions of the world, including their own, are coming together as foretold and a common truth is about to be revealed.

What we continue to learn from our contacts with the various international religions is that there is not one true path to God. There are as many paths as there are lessons to be learned. We can choose a path that teaches a certain truth and wisdom we are missing from our existence. We must choose whatever path brings us closer to God.

6. When God Speaks to You, Follow His Directions

The voice of God is everywhere, in the crack of thunderstorms or the sweet song of a bird. Often we are so busy living that we miss God's voice and fail to learn our life's lessons.

Lakey listened when God sent his angels. He stopped taking drugs and began his mission of helping humankind. He had hit bottom but in less than three years he became internationally known for his talent and for the spirituality associated with his art. Many would shrug off a message from God. Lakey did not and was rewarded with fame and abundance.

Ours is a similar story. We had reached the bottom, lost all our possessions and our livelihood. We received our message from God and acted on it. We were ridiculed by our families, other business owners and many of our customers at the beginning.

Nevertheless, we stuck to our mission, and the more we worked at fulfilling our mission the more successful we became. Our store is now recognized as one of the most successful new businesses in Ventura. We have received national and international media recognition. As any merchant will attest, this is truly miraculous for a store run by people with no past retail experience.

7. Thank God for What You are Given

During a television interview on *City View* in 1996, Lakey said, "I thank God each day for the gifts He has given me."

We all need to thank God for our gifts every day. Andy Lakey is not the only person to receive a gift from God. We all have special abilities that God has given us to fulfill our mission. Sometimes people who have lost their way, like Andy, just need a kick in the pants to recognize their mission. Once this happens, it is important to thank God for the lessons He is teaching us.

Kimberly Clark Sharp, a social worker, related the story of a Long Island, New York attorney in her book, *After the Light*. After his near-death experience he became obsessed with the idea of selling all his belongings and traveling throughout the world, using his money to help others. Ms. Sharp counseled the man at his distressed wife's request. She told him not to act on his message for one year, and he did as she suggested. He eventually developed a different outlook, one which led to a more meaningful solution to the world's problems. He changed the structure of his legal practice and now does a great deal of good for New York's poor through pro bono support of their causes.

Your mission from God might be obvious. It might be what you are doing right now or it could be what you would love to do but have not had the time to do successfully. Whatever it is, trust in God, give it all you have, and you cannot fail.

8. There's More to Life Than Meets the Eye

God is always sending us messages, but we are often so distracted by our own agendas that we ignore or just cannot see what's going on. For people like me, whose thinking can get stuck in science or cultural logic, God is tolerant. He will send me the same messages repeatedly, in all different ways, until I finally catch on.

Many more stories and incidents have occurred at our store than are presented in this book. Often I have rationalized what's right in front of me, choosing to see things as just a coincidence or the product of deluded minds. However, I am becoming more and more aware that there is a great more going on than meets the eye.

One time an apparently blind woman came into the store. She was using a red-tipped white cane and was accompanied by a sighted woman.

"We have a lot of angels here, don't we?" I said to the sighted woman, trying to make polite conversation.

"I really don't like angels," she said, scowling at me. "I'm only here to find a gift for a friend of mine who likes angels."

"Well, if there's anything I can do to help you find what you're looking for, let me know," I said. I then turned to the blind woman.

"We have some paintings in our gallery by Andy Lakey which I think you might enjoy."

"Are you completely stupid and uncaring?" said the

sighted woman, outraged. "Don't you see my friend is blind? She can't enjoy art."

I explained that they were painted in relief and textured, that they are specifically designed so blind people can appreciate them.

"Okay, let's see this art," she said sternly.

As they entered the gallery, the sighted woman shook her head and said, "Oh no, you won't like this. These paintings are modern art."

The blind woman spoke up. "I want to experience this art," she insisted.

I led her to one of the larger paintings and let her feel its textured surface. She began to cry.

"All my life I have heard about paintings, but this is the first time I have ever been allowed to experience one first hand," she said. "This is wonderful."

The sighted woman was dumbstruck. She did not know what to say. I was shown by God that a blind person with faith could see much more than a sighted person without faith.

Conclusion

The Keeper of the Psychomanteum

In the of spring 1997, a past life regression therapist named Terry Nash came to our store and offered me a free session. Ms. Nash felt it was part of her life's mission to do this for me. I had never done anything like this before, but I believe there are no coincidences. There must have been some reason I needed this insight at this point in my life.

She put me into a hypnotic state and my first vision was of The Virgin of Guadalupe. She came to me in a hazy blue cloud. Her head turned one way then the other, as it had in the photograph I took ten years before. Guadalupe gave me a message: to strive for more forgiveness and tolerance in my life. This was followed by a parable about one of my past lives that took place in 18th Century Mexico.

In that life, I had a cold, distant father who caused me

sadness and frustration by controlling my life. He made me run our small rancho at a young age instead of allowing me to have fun as I wished. He also arranged my marriage to a woman I did not love, to form an alliance that would assure our family's prosperity.

In time I gained insights as to how my father's actions were in fact for my own good and for the good of the family. I could forgive my father and understand his reasoning. I learned to tolerate and respect my wife, and to make something positive of our loveless marriage. Despite all the obstacles, I found love and happiness with our children.

I used my knowledge of forgiveness and tolerance to move ahead and change the pattern of life for my children. I did not dominate their lives or force them to marry or work in ways that would only benefit me. With forgiveness and tolerance, a great deal of abundance and love continued to come to me and my family.

This insight into a past life helped me to better understand my present work. I continue to be confronted by religious radicals and scientific professionals who try to control my efforts. They often claim that I have lost my way—or my mind. My background in hard science (anthropology and psychology) only makes this process more difficult. As Our Lady of Guadalupe told me, I need to find more forgiveness and tolerance of negative forces around me. Lakey's art leads me toward this understanding.

Spirituality and Science

One day in the summer of 1996, a man in our gallery was astounded at the feelings in his hands, but he believed there must be a scientific basis for the phenomenon. A chemical engineer, he believed the sensations were caused by the escape of oxygen molecules trapped beneath the twenty coats of acrylic paint.

I took one of the pencil sketches out of the frame and held it in the air as he ran his hand over it. The sensation was still there. True to his scientific training, the engineer came up with an alternate theory. He said what was causing the sensation was the static caused by the carpet.

We took the frameless sketch to the sidewalk in front of our store.

"There's no static electricity in concrete, is there?" I asked.

"No," he assured me.

He ran his hand over the sketch, amazed once again. He could still feel the insistent sensation.

The challenge for many such people is their conflict between *spirituality* and *science.* The conflict itself is logical, since science is not the absolute truth it is sometimes claimed to be. Science is in some respects just another religion trying to explain the universe according to its own data or theories. This is why many scientists can logically deny the existence of the human soul and life after death, despite so many documented cases from reliable sources. In this respect, it can be said that science has not convincingly refuted evidence of a spiritual power that has fed human hope and given solace for thousands of years.

At a family gathering at my sister's home on Thanksgiving Day in 1996, I showed my aunt a Lakey painting. I related to her the unusual events that were happening in our store when people put their hands over these paintings. I told her about eight-year-old Ashley, who had seen her deceased aunt.

"I don't want to hear any more," my aunt interrupted. "This is stupid. I really think you are losing it, Keith," she continued. "It's too bad that an educated person like you can be taken in by all this mumbo jumbo."

I told her the stories were all verifiable. I had names, addresses and phone numbers of the people I was describing.

"I think that little Ashley girl was just brainwashed by her mother and her grandmother," she responded. "And you probably gave her some kind of hypnotic suggestion."

I assured her my data was legitimate. "How do you explain the other eight-year-old girl, the twelve-year-old girl, the police officer's wife or the Native American man all having the same experience?" I asked.

My aunt became even more irate.

"Don't you get it?! They're all just telling you what you want to hear."

"Do you believe in the human soul?" I asked.

"I don't know," she shook her head. "But what you're telling me is really crazy."

She got up and walked away. I felt anger and resentment; I felt like lashing out and calling her names. Instead I composed myself and said, as calmly as possible, "I pray someday you'll find more spirituality in your life."

I sometimes wonder why have I been chosen to pass on this knowledge, because, like Moses, I am a most unlikely prophet. I'm not a very good public speaker and I'm not charismatic. It just seems that it's God's plan. I have literally stumbled upon one miracle after another through a series of meaningful coincidences. I now think of these as my "messages from God."

What I have described on these pages is not an end, but rather a beginning. I need to do more to understand my mission from Our Lady of Guadalupe. I need to do more to find additional forgiveness and tolerance in my life.

My knowledge of science and my ability to convey my experience in logical scientific terms may be the reason I have this mission. Someone with credibility is needed to bring these messages to the world. Only someone as open-minded as I could be the keeper of the Psychomanteum, a magical chamber where religious beliefs can be reaffirmed, a lost loved one may be bid goodbye, or spirituality can be regained.

The next time you are in Ventura, California, drop by our store, *Things from Heaven.* There you can experience the awe, the joy and wonder of God's angels first hand.

I do not find my task burdensome. It is a labor of love. It is my mission from God. I am the keyholder to the sacred room and the teller of the miraculous tales.

I am the keeper of the Psychomanteum.

ORDER FORM

Andy Lakey's Psychomanteum
Spiritual Journeys Guided by Art, Angels and Miracles

ISBN 9961555-0-5 ★ $12.95

Available at bookstores and angel stores everywhere.
Published by Ventura Press

☏ Telephone orders: Call toll free: 1(888)ANGEL17. Please have your Visa or MasterCard ready.

✉ To order by mail, send check or money (no cash or CODs) to: Ventura Press, P.O. Box 662, Ventura, CA 93002-662.

Please send me ________ copy(s) of Andy Lakey's Psychomanteum

I am enclosing $__________

Plus postage & handling* $__________

California residents add 7.25% sales tax $__________

Total amount enclosed $__________

*$2.00 for first book; $1.00 for each additional book

Name ____

Address ____

City ______________________ State _____ Zip _____________

Payment:
☐ Check
☐ Credit card: ☐ Visa ☐ MasterCard

Card number: ____________________________ Exp.date:________

Name on card: ____

Prices and availability subject to change without notice.
Valid in U.S. only.

Wholesale distributors call 1(888)ANGEL17 (264-3517)
for prices and terms.

ORDER FORM

Andy Lakey's Psychomanteum
Spiritual Journeys Guided by Art, Angels and Miracles

ISBN 9961555-0-5 ★ $12.95

Available at bookstores and angel stores everywhere.
Published by Ventura Press

☎ Telephone orders: Call toll free: 1(888)ANGEL17. Please have your Visa or MasterCard ready.

✉ To order by mail, send check or money (no cash or CODs) to: Ventura Press, P.O. Box 662, Ventura, CA 93002-662.

Please send me ________ copy(s) of Andy Lakey's Psychomanteum

I am enclosing $__________

Plus postage & handling* $__________

California residents add 7.25% sales tax $__________

Total amount enclosed $__________

*$2.00 for first book; $1.00 for each additional book

Name ____

Address ____

City ______________________ State _____ Zip ____________

Payment:
☐ Check
☐ Credit card: ☐ Visa ☐ MasterCard

Card number: ____________________________ Exp.date:________

Name on card: ____

Prices and availability subject to change without notice.
Valid in U.S. only.

Wholesale distributors call 1(888)ANGEL17 (264-3517) for prices and terms.